MOM LETOURNEAU

The remarkable story of MOM LeTourneau

Norman B. Rohrer

TYNDALE HOUSE
PUBLISHERS, INC.
WHEATON, ILLINOIS

Third printing, September 1987
Library of Congress Catalog Card Number 84-52399
ISBN 0-8423-4502-7

CONTENTS

FOREWORD
by Shirley Stanfield LeTourneau

Mary Evelyn Peterson LeTourneau, known the world around as "Mom," has written her page of history full. The eloquence of her actions provides direction for women seeking the joy of fulfillment in biblical roles.

Events, rather than extensive schooling, were the tutor of this indomitable woman. With grace she accepted the challenges of swift change, frequent inconvenience, hard toil, the loss of three of her seven children, and the solitude fostered by a workaholic husband.

Mom could have been among the world's most affluent women, but she chose to live an unadorned, almost artless life so that she would have resources for her ministries. She lived by the philosophy that prosperity is from God and must be shared in his name.

Mom became my mother-in-law in 1951 when I married her fourth son, Roy. She was a caring woman and sensed some needs in my life that day she took me to the hospital where I gave birth to our second child.

Roy was in the jungles of Peru setting up our "Bibles and Bulldozers" ministry. For hours she sat by my bed recalling both the good times and the difficulties of her generation. It was a reassuring time for me.

Mom is not a gourmet chef; yet she has fed literally thousands of people in her home, at the factories, and on rural construction jobs, and her recipes, as they appeared in the company newsletter, have been read by millions. She is not trained in business; yet she bought and managed camps, ranches, houses, and lands, and kept neat, balanced books. She is not a preacher; yet her quiet admonitions have endeared her to a global family.

Mom sits much of the time in her chair now, her knees arthritic but her mind clear. She is surrounded by photographs of family and friends, the telephone, note pad, TV, and books. Here she prays for her loved ones and is available to anyone. She will gladly join in with any visitor to sing that favored hymn by William Cowper, "God Moves in a Mysterious Way," with a bit of forgivable improvising:

Ye fearful Moms, fresh courage take;
The clouds ye so much dread
Are big with mercy, and shall break
In blessings on your head.

CHAPTER ONE

THE BRIDE'S ESCAPE

THE August air was hot and still as Evelyn Peterson, sixteen, drifted through the kitchen of her parents' frame house in Stockton, California. She paused at the back door for one last look. Her mother and father were entertaining friends that Sunday afternoon, two brothers and a sister played in the front yard, and baby brother slept. She closed the front door quietly and ran down the sidewalk to her waiting lover.

"You'll need a coat," Bob LeTourneau whispered as Evelyn sprang into his topless touring car.

"I can't go back now," she replied. "Mother will suspect. . . ."

Bob put the Saxon into gear and eased away from the curb. They crept through the city streets, then found the open road leading south.

In the society of 1917, only a rare sixteen-year-old girl would have had the pluck to be portaged across the Mexican border by a garage mechanic twelve years her senior, and be married against the will of her parents. In their agony, Oscar and America Peterson were convinced that their eldest daughter would be a mistress in her youth and a nursemaid in her old age; but matters are not always as troubled parents imagine them to be.

Evelyn had picked her man when she was twelve years old and had never wavered from her love for him. Had her father the same perspective, he might not have fought the marriage to the annulment court or might have thought better about refusing to speak to his son-in-law for seven long years.

It is one of those happy little ironies that Oscar eventually went to work for his son-in-law in the emerging LeTourneau manufacturing operation. Contrary to Oscar's dire predictions, his strong-willed daughter allowed God and her husband to channel her energy and confidence into varied enterprises and exemplary Christian conduct. Her children and people on three continents have risen up to call her blessed.

Had they lived, Oscar and America would have been proud to see her plan the meal and serve as hostess to the seven thousand people who gathered to dedicate a manufacturing plant in Mississippi in 1942. Even Queen Esther might not have done better, for Evelyn had learned from her admiring husband how to think big.

Her parents would have cheered as their daughter with only a year and a half of high school founded an institution of higher learning.

And they would have nodded approval as she purchased one youth camp after another in an attempt to salvage troubled lives and turn them toward God . . . and was chosen "National Mother of the Year" . . . and rode in the flower-bedecked Tournament of Roses float seen around the world.

If you can find a truly good wife, she is worth more than precious gems. Her husband can trust her, and she will richly satisfy his needs. She will not hinder him, but help him all her life. She buys food and serves an army of industrial workers; she considers a field and turns it into a camp for youth; she organizes a technical college and travels across oceans with messages of good news. When she speaks, her words are wise, and kindness is the rule for everything she says. Her children stand and bless her.

—an adaptation from Proverbs 31

CHAPTER TWO

PINAFORE JUNCTION

A GIRL whose youthful feet touch the soil and whose soul breathes in the sweet air of the country under the open face of heaven learns early the necessity of labor—and its fulfilling joy. Since men have written most of our history books, the role of women and mothers in our communities and families has not always been given its due. The Wild West could never have been tamed, the vast prairies plowed, nor God and learning brought to the corners of our continent without the strength, bravery, and influence of our grandmothers, great-grandmothers, and the women who came before them.

Life in Evelyn Peterson's California at the turn of the century bristled with possibilities. The gold rush of 1849 had flourished and died, leaving in its wake dozens of villages with names like You Bet, Rough and Ready, Kaktus Korner, and Mark West Creek.

Mark West Creek, more than a dry wash, was the farming community near Santa Rosa where Evelyn was born on November 15, 1900—the first child of Oscar

William and America Butler Peterson. The quiet, soft-spoken girl seemed unwearied in her youthful responsibilities. There were eggs to gather, cows to milk, and even fields to cultivate, which she did with the best of hirelings.

Mr. Peterson—high-strung, musical, temperamental—moved his family fifteen times and never owned a house. In Stanislaus County, between Manteca and Ripon, he enjoyed some community prestige as the one who hired the marms to teach the next generation in the one-room Calla School. He was constantly trying to find instructors who could teach the three R's to the reluctant offspring of busy farmers. Many of the ranchers would rather have had their youngsters at home to work.

There grew up in the Calla School, which Evelyn attended, a group of big boys who were still in grade school in their teens. These ruffians ran off all the good teachers. So Oscar launched a search for a teacher who could teach to the tune of a hickory stick.

One day out plowing, he observed a young woman coming toward him, leaning into the wind and plodding in high black shoes through the freshly-turned earth.

"Here comes my teacher," Oscar decided.

He hired her on the spot and briefed her about the problem classroom she had inherited. Evelyn was in the school when the new teacher arrived.

"I expect obedience," the newcomer announced as a fair warning, but the big boys assumed they would quickly run this teacher off as they had done the others.

When the first noises began to crescendo from the

rowdy corner, the teacher said not a word. She calmly walked out to her buggy, seized her whip, and strode back inside with every eye focused on her. She lined up five boys in front of their peers and punished them with that whip. For that entire first week she spoke softly and carried her big whip, blistering the backs of anyone who stepped out of line. Each afternoon when Evelyn climbed on her horse and headed home she had a new story to tell her father.

At the grocery store in Manteca, Oscar happened to meet Milo Munson, one of the rowdiest. "Well, Milo," he said, "how do you like your new teacher?"

"Oh, Mr. Peterson," Milo exclaimed, "she's the best we ever had."

"She is?" asked Oscar, surprised. "Does she make you mind?"

"Make us *mind?* Feel my back."

Oscar ran his hand down Milo's back inside his shirt and felt a criss-crossing series of welts. "How come?" he asked.

"Well, we come up against someone we can't run outta that school now," said Milo.

She properly prepared the boys to pass and move on, but she later had a nervous breakdown and had to resign. The base for good behavior was laid at Calla School, but a heavy price had been paid.

Evelyn liked all of her teachers but was extremely shy. She found it impossible to recite in front of the class and would rather take a zero than speak before an audience. She was meticulous and honest. To one math question she was the only one in the class to get it right because she would let no one copy her work.

There is little recorded about Evelyn's romances among the youthful suitors for two reasons: the girl who could give the teacher answers to mathematical quizzes was a girl too strong for the average boy. The other reason was Robert Gilmour LeTourneau. Though for four years she watched him through her tears as he dated other girls, she had a certitude that he was the one to whose care and keeping she would dedicate her life.

Farms and ranches are among the most dangerous places to grow up, but the Peterson five (Evelyn, Ray, Howard, Edna, and Buster) survived. One Saturday morning stands out in the Peterson book of memories. Evelyn, eleven years old, had hitched up old Granny to the spring wagon as she usually did on the last day of the week, and made for town with three younger children and a grocery list to stock the larder for the week.

When she arrived back home she found her mother in bed with wet cloths on her face, moaning for a doctor. America had tried to light a kerosene burner that her husband had rigged into the wood-burning cookstove. The obstinate flame had flickered weakly and refused to warm the kettle. She had just rammed a poker into the firebox when the stove exploded in her face.

America's eyebrows and eyelashes had disappeared; the front of her hair was black from soot, and her face was badly burned. The baby she carried was later born dead and with malformed eyes. Evelyn jumped into the wagon and raced back to town. The doctor sent her home with some ointment.

America survived this and other accidents, but she

never fully recovered from overexertion under a hot sun on the farm one afternoon. While helping Oscar in the fields, she spotted a ditch breaking up and shoveled so intensely that she went home with a sunstroke and never tolerated sunshine well again.

A year later the Petersons moved to Stockton. The city gave them more possibilities for friendships and closer associations than the rural environment could offer. It also moved them closer to kinfolk. Evelyn at one time had the family tree nearly completely charted on paper. However, she needed additional information from the matriarchal Aunt Bell on the ranch at Mark West Creek. Her aunt died before Evelyn obtained the records. Her uncle promised to send them, but fire destroyed the homestead and also took the recorded lineage.

The reader of this record may be just as happy not to be treated to long lists of Swedes and British emigrants of another generation. Suffice it to say that America's maiden name was Butler and her maternal grandmother's name was Sutliff, a hardy woman who had traveled west to California a generation earlier at the time of the 1849 gold rush.

Stockton gave Oscar ideas for a new business. He built wooden frames to launder lace curtains for hotels and the carriage trade. Evelyn's morning duty before school was to wash the curtains and stretch them on frames. After school she would take them off the frames and iron the pin holes out. To repair rotten fabric she would take assorted pieces from disintegrating curtains and dip them into cold starch and water. These she would lay over the old, torn curtains and iron them in place. When the curtains were finished and folded carefully, she would wrap them in bundles larger than she, carry them half a block to the streetcar, and deliver them.

Evelyn had little time for anything else but her school and the curtain business. Her father measured the curtains and set the frames, but Evelyn did the rest. Oscar had become a teamster, working for a transfer company in the city.

Until the summer of 1913, when Evelyn was twelve, her religious training was sadly lacking. She perfunctorily attended the Plymouth Brethren assembly with her parents, but no stirring of the Spirit was evident. This year evangelists Hillis and Greerson pitched a gospel tent at Main and Sierra Nevada Streets. The Plymouth Brethren made a point to visit each home among the membership. They had noticed in the services that "young Evelyn appears to be under conviction of sin." The evangelists asked America if they might speak to the girl alone. Evelyn, upstairs eavesdropping, panicked.

"Mother called me into the parlor, but I sneaked into the kitchen instead, scared to death to talk to those austere men. But Mother persisted and I went."

The kind men opened the Bible and spoke to Evelyn alone. She listened, then cried, then prayed.

"That was the day of my conversion. I accepted the Lord as my Savior. When I ran to the kitchen to tell Mother, I was so happy I felt as though my feet hadn't even touched the floor."

This emotional outburst was unusual for the level-headed eldest daughter. It was an experience she never forgot. Too timid to evangelize by herself, she would make candy and give it to any children who would go with her to church where the minister could present the whole counsel of God and draw the net.

Something else of consequence happened in the little Plymouth Brethren tent at Main and Sierra Nevada Streets: Evelyn first met Bob LeTourneau, a cocky young nonconformist who was the fourth child of eight children born to Caleb Thucydides LeTourneau and his wife, Elizabeth Lorimer LeTourneau. Bob was twenty-four, so he paid little attention to the twelve-year-old girl in the congregation. His salvation had transformed his soul, but his blustery approach to life remained characteristic. He thought big . . . bigger . . . biggest, and many a mechanic who laughed at his ideas later had to admit that the LeTourneau design was best.

From the edge of town the Petersons moved to the larger quarters of 22 North Sierra Nevada Street. Bob showed up frequently for a good home-cooked dinner and some fun with the kids. When he broke his neck being thrown through a fence while racing an automobile they were his chief commiserators. His head ever afterward listed to the right.

"Bob," Oscar said one day when the young man was back on his feet, "you're sleeping on that cot over there in your garage. We've got an extra room. Why don't you move in?"

With those kind words Oscar gained a boarder and lost his daughter, but the camaraderie between them lasted for four fat years before the seven lean ones prevailed.

CHAPTER THREE

SHE PICKS HER MATE

THE new boarder was an instant hit at the Petersons' home—race car driver, garage mechanic, and innovator. With pretended disdain he would survey the boyish toys of Howard and Ray, but clap them on the back when he approved of a contraption that he thought might work.

Bob LeTourneau (R.G.) liked to drive the Petersons to Snowline for picnics and treat them to ice cream on hot summer nights. Bashful Evelyn gave him sidelong looks of love, but he took no notice.

After two years of this, Evelyn reached the age of fourteen. Each time Bob dressed for a date she would polish his shoes, see that his necktie was straight, and make sure he left the house well groomed. When he was gone she would flee to her room and cry, praying that the Lord would "save him for me."

Evelyn liked to ride with Bob when he delivered automobiles or tested them after an engine had been repaired. She liked to sit with him in church and listen to his booming voice singing hymns in the choir.

Alice Gilmour, the daughter of Bob's father's friend after whom R.G. received his middle name, dated Bob occasionally, but even the thickest head would eventually take note of the excessive fussing of this little girl in her eagerness to attend to his grooming.

"Do you care if I go out with Alice Gilmour?" Bob asked her one enchanted evening.

Evelyn shrugged.

"Would you care if I married her?" he asked.

Evelyn said nothing.

"Would you *really* care?" Bob pressed.

"Yes, I would," Evelyn declared with sudden boldness.

Thus she bound him to her. It was the only proposal she ever got, but she was satisfied with it. After all, those three little words knocked Alice Gilmour out of the nuptial aisle and some sense into that stubborn head of R.G. LeTourneau, the genius heading for world renown.

A rich girl he was not marrying (she had three dresses to her name). Her father's permission he could not ask for, upon threat of the judge's chambers for Bob. Oscar wanted his daughter to wait until she was eighteen. When neighbors heard what happened next, how the young boarder had stolen Oscar and America Peterson's daughter away, not one in a hundred would have given the marriage more than a fifty-fifty chance.

The magic evening of their attempt to elope was calm in late fall when Bob drove his four-cylinder Saxon touring car to a back street where Evelyn was waiting.

They wound through the familiar streets of Stockton, then headed for the main highway leading south to Mexico where they would be married. The fog was thick, so when they reached a hotel in Madera, they stopped for the night. Bob called his garage in Stockton and told the night boy to call the Petersons and tell them he and Evelyn would be back in a few days. Oscar and his son Ray went to the garage and borrowed one of Bob's cars for the pursuit. Oscar called the telephone operator and found out that the call had come from a hotel in Madera, so the father and son left about midnight to try to find them.

The offended father seemed to smell the trail. He pushed the throttle of the Regal sedan to the vibrating floorboards in hot pursuit. He traced his daughter to an obscure hotel in Madera where Evelyn and Bob were sleeping discreetly on separate floors in separate rooms. With the passkey supplied by the hotel management, Oscar slipped quietly into Evelyn's room and ordered her to get dressed. She was going home.

After that, the boarder's bed was moved out of the Peterson house and the door of hospitality was closed. "Bob," Oscar threatened, "Evelyn can never see you again." But he finally softened and allowed her to go out with him.

By August 27, 1917, the risk of romantic adventures had passed, or so Evelyn's parents thought. America was upstairs with her sewing . . . Oscar was telling jokes to his cronies on the front porch . . . Evelyn was quietly rocking her baby brother to sleep. Into this peaceful scene once again crept that Saxon touring car.

The baby slept after three attempts to settle him; the flies buzzed; suppertime approached, and the family gathered for dinner.

"Evelyn?"

This time the Saxon was heading down the coastal route to avoid the father's wrath. This time it would roll all night. Bob had brought along plenty of spare tires and tools to keep his stallion on the gallop. He picked up a hitchhiker to avoid suspicion by officers who might be searching for them.

By midmorning the second day, as the couple approached the U.S.-Mexico border, they spotted the dreaded barricade. Had Oscar finally caught them again? But their papers were in order, and the officers let them pass. The law wanted an escaped bank robber, not two young lovers who that day would pledge their troth and drive a stake that would anchor them for fifty-two years.

In Tijuana, Bob found a humble house with the shingle announcing *Capilla de Casamiento*—Justice of the Peace. The only documentation needed was quickly produced: the groom was twenty-eight, the bride sixteen, both citizens of the United States of America.

The sweet smiles of love on their faces were not reflected by their scattered family members. The outsmarted Oscar Peterson was livid with rage. Caleb and Elizabeth LeTourneau, along with Bob's brothers and sisters, had moved to Long Beach, which was the first stop of the newlyweds en route home.

R.G.'s mother made the remark, "Well, I'm not happy that Bob is married to that little girl, but he *is* married and so we'll treat 'em with love."

As Mr. and Mrs. Robert G. LeTourneau drove up to the curb, Caleb came out to the car and asked, "Where's the license?" Phil, Bob's youngest brother, produced a frontpage clipping from the *Stockton Record* headlined, "Prominent Automobile Dealer Elopes with 16-year-old Girl."

By the end of that week Bob and Evelyn drove into Stockton to face the music. Oscar was at the livery stable when they arrived. Bob drove to the back street again. Evelyn knew her father would be mad, "but I didn't know *how* mad, so I didn't want Bob to go with me into the house."

She walked a block down the street and into the kitchen. Just as she stepped inside her father phoned from work.

"Guess who just got here," America spoke into the telephone.

Oscar hung up and started to run toward home, stopping only long enough to pick up a crony named Cornwall. Oscar stormed into the house and confronted his daughter.

"You will not leave this house again until you are eighteen years old, if I have to stay home and guard you myself!" he shouted.

He and Cornwall went into the front bedroom by themselves to decide what their next move should be. Her brother Ray arrived home from school at about the same time; so Evelyn told him to run out the back gate and tell Bob to bring the car to Ophir Street beside the little horse barn. When Bob pulled up, Evelyn sneaked out the back door, jumped into the open car, and disappeared while her father was on the telephone with the district attorney.

Good to his word, Oscar swore out a warrant for Bob's arrest on the charge that he had contributed to the delinquency of a minor.

"Mr. LeTourneau," the judge intoned on the day of arraignment, "just when was it that you told Evelyn what you planned to do?"

"Well, your honor, we had just turned the corner. . . . No, I remember that I told her before we left to go back into the house and get a coat, but she said, 'No, my mother would get wise if I took out my coat on a warm day.'"

The judge said, "I think she knew what she was doing," and dismissed the case.

Oscar had been devastated, first by his daughter and now by the law. In this powerless state, chafing against the weakness he felt, he approached his son-in-law: "Bob, I'll never speak to you again." He would have sworn on a Bible that he meant to carry out his decision. But time, grandchildren, and the softening of years work on aging men and give them some seasoning, so that "never . . . again" was shortened to seven awkward years. At the end of the "famine" Oscar Peterson put out his hand: "Bob, let's bury the hatchet." For the rest of his life, Oscar worked for R.G. LeTourneau and made a good wage.

Evelyn LeTourneau always felt "liberated" as the wife of a man who would one day become world famous for his inventions. She wanted only to help her husband to succeed, to be comfortable. All of their married life she daily laid out his suits, shirts, ties, socks, and shoes. One day when she had sprained her foot, she asked, "Pop, would you get my crutches out of the closet?" R.G. asked, "Where's the closet?"

Evelyn always called the barber to make appointments for his haircuts. His sons had to drive him to the bank one day to sign papers because R.G. had no idea where it was; the man didn't even know for sure how much he made. "Mom," he asked one day, "how much is my paycheck each month?"

One morning as he sat down to breakfast she asked, "How do you like your new suit?"

R.G. looked down at his sleeve. "Oh," he said, "I guess it is new, isn't it?"

At the age of twelve she thought Bob LeTourneau was "wonderful," and she never changed her opinion of him in the fifty-two years of their married life.

CHAPTER FOUR

ONE LITTLE . . .
TWO LITTLE . . .

B Y now the couple had been blessed (or cursed) with a certain degree of notoriety in the city, in the church, and among the neighbors. This wait-and-see attitude among the skeptical can enlarge the determination of a young couple to see it through. However, there seem to have been no quarrels to patch up, no stormy period of adjustment. The two personalities meshed like the cogs of Bob's machinery. But World War I was lurking, and the groom would soon be called to war.

He didn't have to travel far. The naval base at Mare Island in Susun Bay needed mechanical technicians. Bob needed no summons. In January 1918 he bundled up his bride and took her with him, depositing her in the best quarters available in the town of Vallejo—a ramshackle country house on twenty acres. While Bob was "at war," Evelyn peeled off crusts of dirt (actually shoveled dirt and debris out of the house), sewed curtains, laid linoleum, and painted the woodwork.

At six o'clock each morning R.G. left the honeymoon cottage and arrived back twelve hours later for dinner. Evelyn purchased a cow, tended a brood of turkeys, and had the use of the old Saxon.

On November 15 that year Evelyn turned eighteen. While many of her peers were giggling at parties, having their first dates, or thinking of the Senior Prom at high school, Evelyn was making a home, tending a small farm, keeping the books, managing the money, and praying for children to fill her house.

Oscar would have been secretly proud to see his daughter cruising the meadow in that big car to nudge the reluctant bovine toward home with the bumper so she could be milked. Life was beautiful right in the midst of war.

In late October, when the summer heat of 1918 had passed, Evelyn prepared to give birth to her firstborn. Bob took her to the Gilmours' house in Stockton to await her maternity appointment at Rickers Sanitarium.

Overshadowing this happy scene, a terrifying epidemic of deadly influenza spread across the nation. Bob went back to work, and Evelyn waited impatiently to be delivered. Should she risk entering Rickers Sanitarium on Washington Street where the doctor had agreed to deliver her baby for $25? Would she be exposing her child to influenza?

As Evelyn was making her decision, word came that R.G. had fallen victim to the flu on Mare Island. He was not expected to live through the night. An alert doctor found him in time to inject a shot of potent liquid to induce sweating. The procedure worked; R.G.

began to perspire and managed to sweat away the fever on his way to recovery.

Two nurses died at Rickers Sanitarium, and several of the patients had caught the flu germ. So Evelyn's doctor made her decision for her: she would have her baby on the guest bed at the Gilmours' house. She couldn't go to her parents' home because her little brother had also caught the flu.

In the evening of October 30, 1918, while his father lay close to death, little Caleb Thomas entered this world, the first of seven children to be born to the LeTourneaus. Twelve days later the Armistice was signed and the war ended. The new mother called her husband's sister Sarah in Long Beach and asked her to take care of R.G. in their Vallejo house when he returned from the hospital. On November 10 the new father arrived home. The doctor let him come to the door of the room where his son was born, but he could get no closer.

After R.G. had seen his baby, two of the Gilmour daughters caught the flu. The doctor told Evelyn to take her baby out of that house. She called her friend Nellie Pierson. Together they found an apartment near the hospital. While Sarah took care of Bob in Vallejo, Nellie made sure that Evelyn had food in order to nurse her baby. From that apartment window, all alone, Evelyn watched the hearses night after night as they carried away the dead who had been struck down by the epidemic. Bob and Sarah loaded a trailer with the LeTourneaus' earthly goods and moved back to Stockton.

What joy reunion brings. When neighbors gathered

to see the baby, they must have remarked—with that extravagant liberty we allow ourselves on such occasions—that Caleb Thomas was a pretty big handle for such a sweet little cherub to carry, and that if he could handle it as a baby, what fine things must be in store for the lad.

"Give the boy a superior mother," A. W. Tozer said in his biography of A. B. Simpson, "and he will make the grade somehow."

During those first few months of Caleb's life, his mother stole many an admiring glance at the wee boy with the round head and large round eyes. But the epidemic hung on, and somewhere, somehow, little Caleb met the germ and was destroyed by it. After just one hundred days, on February 9, 1919, he was torn from his mother's breast, wrenched from his father's dreams, and returned to heaven to await them.

Harry A. Ironside conducted the funeral. Bob and Evelyn didn't have a nickel to give him then. But years later they would make up for it.

R.G. returned with leaden feet to the garage business he had left behind in Stockton, where he was in for another shock. While he had been away, his partner had borrowed heavily on the company's resources to finance a love affair and had failed to pay back the bank on time. When the erring businessman refused to marry the girl he had courted, she sued him for a sum equivalent to everything he owned. He had sold a lot of cars, but had spent the money on his lady love instead of paying off the debts. Now the business stood at the point of bankruptcy.

The bank assembled the creditors. It was decided

that if the LeTourneaus could raise five thousand dollars, the partner could have the business, and Bob would be free. The creditors were giving Bob and Evelyn an opportunity to buy out of the business, so his partner could be given another chance.

The business crisis was easily resolved; the loss of their son was not. Evelyn pondered God's piteous providence and found relief in her tears. Her stalwart husband groaned in his grief and cried out with that booming voice for help from the God of all comfort.

When he got up from his knees he came to his senses. "We have lived for material things," R.G. reminded his wife as he stood beside Caleb's empty bed. "We haven't given God his rightful place."

Here began the turning-point, an adjustment in two lives that was to test the principle of gaining by giving, of proving the biblical principle that states that the liberal shall prosper, and "he that watereth shall be watered again."

For half a century Evelyn and Bob would practice giving good gospel measure, pressed down, shaken together, and running over. Fifteen years later the LeTourneaus would set aside 90 percent of their company's stock and designate it for the Lord's work, thus giving up an opportunity to be numbered among the exceedingly affluent of this world.

Perhaps Caleb, the wee boy with the big name, had come for that purpose alone. Perhaps one hundred days were enough for him to accomplish his mission. Strange and wonderful are the ways of God.

After the settlement with the creditors at the garage, R.G. went out to find employment. A friend told him about a large farm in the Island District not far from Stockton. The farmer needed someone to overhaul his Holt tractor. "I know you could do it, Bob," his friend affirmed.

R.G. had never been near a Holt tractor, but he figured it couldn't be much different from an automobile, so he went to take a look. The farmer offered him a job at six dollars per day plus his keep.

"Well," R.G. drawled, "I'll tell you what. I'll work one week for you. If I'm not worth eight dollars a day, I'll leave and you won't owe me a cent."

He worked one week, pocketed the eight dollars per day, and stayed all summer. When he had the tractor running, the farmer said, "Go plow that field next to the barn." R.G. didn't know how to drive the tractor, so he quickly had his helper show him how to shift and how to turn a square corner so as not to leave weeds in the corners of the field.

To fill the empty hours, Mom found a job across the river from her groom. She learned about a woman who was planning a trip to Europe for the summer and who wanted someone to take her place caring for two small children—one the age that Caleb would have been. Like Miriam of old, Evelyn "sat by the river, and drew in the basket." Upon this surrogate child, she lavished her love. The second child was nine months old.

All that season Evelyn lived in the big house on the bank of the river, bought her groceries from a floating market on a riverboat that docked nearby, and lived for the moments when her husband would visit.

To reach his wife twice a week, Bob would drive a mile to the river, undress in the bulrushes, tie his clothes in a bundle, put them on a log, and push it in front of him as he swam across the river. Then he would dress on the opposite shore. To speed up the process of getting home, he welded a couple of pontoons to a piece of sheet metal and rowed across. This saved him sixteen miles of land travel around the island.

The woman returned from Europe at summer's end and Evelyn joined her husband, who was then living in a sugar shack near his fields. Daylight shined in through the cracks of her "house," and the wind blew dust over dishes and linens. In the morning before opening their eyes they had to brush aside the sand and grit. She set her table with the plates upside down, and when it was time to turn them over and ladle on the food, tiny patterns of dust could be seen on the table cloth. This lasted until Christmas when they closed the shack for good and traveled to Long Beach where they enjoyed Christmas with the LeTourneaus.

In Long Beach R.G. borrowed enough money from his sister Sarah to buy a tractor like the Holt he had fixed and worked on the farm. This contraption put him in business for himself, and he could be seen for many months leveling land around Stockton in a cloud of dust.

At noon on April 2, 1920, Evelyn gave birth to her second child, a daughter she named Sarah Louise. Mom's husband came in from the job he was working on thirty miles from home. He stayed long enough to kiss his wife, meet his wee daughter, and receive congratulations. Then he headed back to work. Deep in his heart, R.G. might have feared that his life of wheels, grease, engines, and dirt would be wasted on a girl.

Louise, as one might expect in the fortuities of life, surprised him. She seemed fashioned for the sake of innocent mischief. If she wasn't sliding across the kitchen floor on a pound of butter, she was plastering the butter on the wall.

One time her mother heard a scream in the backyard and ran to investigate. There was Louise, holding one end of a snake while her dog was holding the other end—the growling mutt shaking his head, trying to get the prize for himself, Louise screaming for him to let go because she wanted the reptile for herself.

One daughter in a house full of boys has her share of unhappy memories. She longed for the sister who never came and was not made happy when her father bounded out of the house en route back to work after seeing her fifth brother, Ben, for the first time and exclaimed, "Hot dog, I've got me another cat skinner."

Louise's mother's preference for boys and her camps catering to boys did little to assuage the girl's longing for approval and affirmation. Today, as a widow, Louise lives in Longview, Texas, near her mother, coming the full circle of family love to make a new beginning with another widow.

Evelyn's lone vigil at home with her baby girl was a harbinger of the life-style she would endure for all of her married life. She adapted gladly, as youth adapts in love, and later as maturity adapts through understanding.

Pop's work was his recreation. She watched him sketch his mechanical adaptations, sometimes using the dust on the driveway in front of the house. She noticed the wiggling of his foot whenever he mentally sketched his mechanical drawings that eventually produced a steady stream of bigger, faster, and more expensive earth-moving monsters.

It was LeTourneau who first thought of putting an electric motor on every wheel of a grader . . . LeTourneau who first used giant rubber tires on tractors and graders . . . LeTourneau who kept frustrating the workers on his assembly line by continually adapting to make his family of machines even better.

For fifty years Mom answered the question, "How do you stand your husband's long absences?" The overworked question always received an enthusiastic reply: "I'd rather have a happy husband part of the time than an unhappy husband all of the time."

She patiently listened to R.G.'s jokes. One told of a banker with a glass eye. The banker said to his customer, "I'll give you a loan if you can tell which is my glass eye."

"It's your left eye," the customer replied.

"How could you tell?" the astonished banker wanted to know.

"Well, I detected in that left eye just a hint of human kindness," came the reply.

Mom, who can't whistle or sing, did enjoy some ability in painting. She found her chief mission, however, in serving. She was never patient with books, preferring action to ease. When Louise was still a toddler, she bundled her up and tagged along with the LeTourneau construction crew, cooking with improvised mobile pots for R.G. and his men in the most cramped and primitive conditions.

By stretching a bit, the LeTourneaus bought an acre

of ground on Moss Avenue in Stockton. On it stood an old house and a barn, the small shed not counted. Evelyn, who had renovated several "sheds" in her three years of marriage, at last had a respectable house with a pump at the sink.

"Isn't it *wonderful?*" she exuded to her sister, Edna, who had come to help her make the old place habitable. Edna, however, shook her head curiously as her sister kept fastening paper to the rough-hewn walls. "I can't see too much that's wonderful," she replied.

"But it's *ours,*" Evelyn reminded her.

"How much did it cost?"

"Three thousand dollars, but we didn't have to pay anything down. Only thirty dollars a month."

Four months after the LeTourneaus took over the house on Moss Avenue, Donald Phillip was born on September 29, 1921. Later came Richard Howard (1925), Roy Samuel (1929), Ted Lorimer (1932), and Ben Walter (1934)—the last two born in their house on Cherokee Lane in Stockton. Their family was complete, but one would be snatched away in his youth by a tragic accident and another would die in his maturity at fifty.

CHAPTER FIVE

MOVING HEAVEN WHILE POP MOVED EARTH

AS William Carey advanced upon India and as Livingstone upon Africa, so Evelyn LeTourneau confronted the spiritual needs of Stockton in 1921 after she moved into their house on Moss Avenue. There was no church for miles and no effort being made to evangelize the families—especially the children. Big sister Evelyn had earned the title of evangelist when at twelve she had made candy to lure the unconverted to Sunday school held in the Peterson home on Lord's Day afternoons. This fervor never left her.

Now as a grown woman she began calling on the neighbors and asking them if the children could come to Sunday school "if I pick them up."

Most of the parents readily agreed to the idea. Evelyn mapped out a route and stacked the children two-deep in her Saxon. Her husband later welded together a flat-bed springless trailer and installed two long benches with backs. He kept the big tires soft so the youngsters wouldn't be thrown off at every bump.

Evelyn would hitch the trailer to her car each Sunday morning and transport the children to the Christian and Missionary Alliance Church, which she and her husband had joined when they moved to town. Some thirty youngsters were her regular charges, and from 1921 to 1935 she bussed the neighborhood contingent to Sunday school.

Most American men are possessive about their automobiles, and her mechanic husband was no different. The year he bought a new Model T Ford, pride got in the way of his spirituality.

"Here," he told Evelyn when he drove it home, "file this service manual. I'm not going to teach you how to drive this one because you're always gone with the car when I need it."

Evelyn had learned to drive on a gear-shift car when she was fourteen years old. But before she filed the manual, she read it from start to finish and discovered how to operate the foot gears of Henry Ford's pride. The next Sunday morning when her husband came looking for his car after singing in the choir, it had been moved.

"Well," she explained, "I had to take the kids home from Sunday school, didn't I?"

Neither Evelyn nor her husband had anything remarkable to report in the realm of physical endurance. Both wanted eight hours of sleep a night, three square meals, and rest on Sunday. The prolific work they accomplished grew out of constant effort and unflagging zeal.

In the area of spiritual commitment they did have something remarkable: both were more content to give generously to the Lord's work than to spend it on themselves. Each year on faith promise Sunday at the Christian and Missionary Alliance Church they pledged five thousand dollars for missions.

But even Peter looked down at the waves in the moment of his greatest burst of faith, and when the economic depression struck in the early thirties, the LeTourneaus saw those waves and were tempted to leave their pledge card blank, contributing only as the Lord enabled. Before church that night they had agreed, "Since we can't meet the payroll at the plant we won't pledge anything to missions this year."

The time for pledging came. Bob was in the choir, Evelyn in a pew with the children. Their minds undoubtedly were focused on their overdue debts. But a small voice spoke to the husband: "Just put me on your payroll."

"But Lord, even if they don't read off names, they give the amounts, and if I do that the whole congregation will know who it is when the pledges are announced." (Others never made pledges that large.)

"You can make several smaller pledges in the names of each one of your children and your wife," the voice urged.

"All right, Lord, I'll put you on the payroll," R.G. decided. He smiled at his wife. All was well. Evelyn remembers, "It wasn't three weeks until our debt was straightened out and we met our payroll." Never afterward did they fail to meet a payroll, although in later years they came precariously close.

R.G. was teaching a Sunday school class of teenage boys at the church. As the summer approached, Evelyn formed the idea of taking his class to Mount Hermon Conference Center in the Santa Cruz Mountains of coastal California.

"Why not?" R.G. boomed.

Evelyn hooked up the trailer and met the six boys at a predetermined spot. This 1932 adventure marked her first in a career of missionary outreach to boys. Louise, Don, Rich, Roy, and Ted were part of the first group. Each of the teenagers held one of the LeTourneau kids. Evelyn cooked enough food for about a week and stored it in a portable pantry, along with a baby buggy for Ted, on the long trailer. She also paid the registration fee for each boy, after extracting from him a promise that he would attend both meetings every day. In return she would fix their meals and take them to the nearby Santa Cruz beach to swim every afternoon.

On the final day, at Sunday breakfast in the mountains, Evelyn took inventory. Only one of the six boys was a Christian. But when her husband came up later that day he led all the rest to the Lord. Evelyn had brought a trailer load of devil-may-care youngsters and was taking home six bright promises for the kingdom of God.

The next year she enrolled twenty-three for the trailer trip to Mount Hermon. Her brother Buster wanted to go, but Evelyn was apprehensive.

"You've got to promise me," she told her youngest brother, who was starting to run with a fast gang, "that you'll be in both meetings every day."

Buster thought it over. "Is it OK if Clarence comes, too?"

"If your buddy can promise me the same thing, yes."

Evelyn kept her fingers crossed for those two, but she need not have worried. Clarence sought her out one evening after the service and said, "Evelyn, I must talk to you."

They found a place at an outdoor table where Clarence poured out a repentant heart. "I want to be saved," he said.

"Do you understand what it means to give your heart to the Lord?" Evelyn asked.

Clarence nodded.

She recited verses from the Scriptures, and Clarence was ready to embrace every promise. Meanwhile, Buster had gone back to the cabin and found a counselor because he too wanted to become a Christian.

The following summer yielded a special trophy. Clarence's older brother Roy was a truck driver for the LeTourneau company but had begun drinking so badly he was let go. R.G., in the meantime, had purchased a truck and found seats for it in an abandoned street car.

"Let's invite Roy to go along to Mount Hermon," Evelyn suggested at the beginning of summer. "Maybe even let him drive the truck."

"OK, if you think he can stay sober," R.G. agreed.

Evelyn prayed devotedly for Roy at Mount Hermon. She watched him in the meetings and with the others on the beach.

"I'll never corner you," she had promised each of the boys. "I'll never try to talk to you against your will, if you'll promise you'll come talk to me when you're ready."

Two nights passed. After devotions Roy hurried up

43

to Evelyn, agitated in his spirit. He grabbed her arm so tightly it hurt, but she said nothing as he led her to a bench out of earshot of the cabin. *He's not been drinking,* Evelyn determined. *I hope he doesn't ask to go home.*

"Evelyn," Roy said, "I can't go on like this. I want to be saved."

Far into the night she talked with Roy. His repentance was genuine, and he became a believer.

Back home, his friends could hardly believe it was the same old Roy who had returned from the Christian camp. He remained sober for months until some of his old cronies persuaded him to drink a few rounds with them. By the time it was midnight Roy was drunk, attempting to find his way home.

Clarence rapped on the LeTourneaus' bedroom window at about one in the morning and called, "Evelyn, can you come over? Roy just came home and he's drunk."

Evelyn jumped out of bed, told her husband where she was going, dressed, and followed Clarence home. She found Roy in the kitchen where his mother was trying to bandage a scratched arm. She was fumbling terribly, so Evelyn sat down beside her, motioned for her to stop and took over, bandaging the wound.

"Evelyn," Roy groaned in his drunkenness, "why are you so nice to me? You know I'm drunk."

"Yep, I know it, Roy."

"Well then, what are you doing all this for?"

"Because I want to see you really come to know the Lord, Roy. The Lord can help you if you'll just ask him to."

44

The rest of the family went to bed while Roy and Evelyn talked. The kindness was remembered by the alcoholic. He never got drunk again that she knew about. The family later moved to Idaho and out of touch.

In December 1970, a minister in New York heard a local radio station announce that Mrs. R.G. Le-Tourneau was coming to town. The minister attended her meeting and afterward told her, "I thought you'd like to meet one of your boys from Mount Hermon days." (He was one of the first six.) The man had served on the mission field for several years and was now a pastor in New York.

Even today, the fruit of Mom's labors continues in the lives of many who found the way through the faithful witness of this willing servant.

CHAPTER SIX

SERVING MAKETH A HAPPY WIFE

WHILE R.G. LeTourneau was taking contracting jobs, building his construction company, and designing machinery that would make LeTourneau a household word, Evelyn developed resourcefulness at home. She made a career of serving her happy man. She managed the house, purchased his clothing and laid out each morning what he would wear, taught herself to drive their Model T Ford, and ran errands. When she needed curtain rods she used R.G.'s tobin bronze welding rods, which he cut to the perfect size.

But with resourcefulness comes the need to adapt. One day as she drove up with a car full of groceries, she noticed that her curtains had all disappeared from the windows. Inside she quickly saw why: R.G. had run out of welding rods, gone into the house, whisked the curtain rods out of their brackets, and let the lace fall to the floor in a heap. Evelyn got back into the Ford, went to the dime store, and bought more rods, making certain that they were not made of tobin bronze.

If Evelyn LeTourneau seems too stable, too self-reliant, too incredibly satisfied with inconveniences, let it be noted that women's finery and leisure pursuits had not the appeal that they might have had to other females. If her husband's plane was leaving in five minutes, she could be ready; if he was on a remote mountain scraping up clouds of dust, she was out there eating it with him.

In the early twenties when Mom was carrying Richard, her fourth child, R.G. bid for and got the job of backfilling the trench for the Hetch-Hetchie Pipe Line that brings water from the lofty Sierra Nevada Mountains into the San Francisco Bay cities. She bundled Louise and Donald into the car and hitched up an enclosed house trailer, which she packed with cooking gear. This she dragged to the heights where she found some tableland and set up camp. Even though she was ill every morning, she forced herself to arise because her men had to eat and she wanted to make sure they ate well. She was not distracted by nutrition necessarily, since the topic was scarcely discussed in those days. Meat, vegetables, salad, and sugary desserts, with plenty of hot coffee to pour—what else could a good meal want?

Out on the pipeline, Mom laundered her clothing at a spring, kept her children occupied, set a full table for every meal, and kept the pots bubbling with hearty fare. She did the same for the crew at the Fillbrook Dam near Marysville, several hundred miles farther north. A toilet was a hole in the ground with a board from tree to tree, enclosed by a piece of canvas. She heated water on an outdoor stove for the occasional baths, which were carried out in a community washtub. She picked wild gooseberries and made jam, jelly, and gooseberry pies.

When the chill of autumn was too much for outside bathing and eating, she bought a big tent and had a wooden floor put down with a stove in the middle for heat and cooking. There she kept house until the snows sent wife and children home to Stockton.

Mom patched up skinned and bruised limbs, went to the side of ailing wives, and took care of loose children picked up in the enlarging community of construction workers. She rushed her brother Ray to the hospital when he fell into the workings of a scraper that crushed his leg.

In 1924 Oscar Peterson extended his hand of friendship and acceptance to his son-in-law, R.G. On January 3, 1925, Richard Howard was born. As a baby of six months he contracted whooping cough, which developed quickly into spinal meningitis. Many were Mom's nightly vigils watching her boy in the oxygen tent built over his bassinet. To nurse him she couldn't take him out of the tent, so she would lean over and stand near while the baby was nourished at her breast.

The doctor determined that Rich "has had this fever too long. I don't think he'll last the night. If he does, he'll never be normal."

Mom and R.G. knelt, as good parents do in their extremities, and put their arms around their son. "Lord," Mom whispered, "he's yours. If Rich can live and be a blessing, please heal him. If he can't and he will never be normal, then we'd rather you take him now."

By sunrise the fever had broken. In a few days the crisis had passed. Rich grew up to be a scholar, seldom taking a book home to study but earning the highest grades of any of the children. He eventually earned his doctoral degree and became president of LeTourneau College.

In 1927, Henry Kaiser climbed a mountain and watched R.G. at work. Back and forth went the machinery, chewing, clawing, hauling, and whittling away at the brown earth.

"R.G.," one of the workmen said, flagging down his scraper, "that's Henry Kaiser up there watching you."

R.G. shut down his rig, walked up, and introduced himself.

"You recognize a good deal when you see it?" Kaiser asked.

"I think so," replied the inventor.

"Then come down to my office and let's talk."

Henry Kaiser bought one of LeTourneau's machines, liked it, and later bought them all, including their patents, for fifty thousand dollars. He also bought all of R.G's tools and his shop—presumably, the family concluded afterward, so that R.G. would spend his time building machines for Kaiser rather than inventing new ones in his own shop.

When R.G. told Mom about the encounter, she didn't have to ask what his answer was. Fifty thousand dollars was more money than she thought there was in the world. She just started packing. Six months later Kaiser made R.G. a subcontractor on a job. The inventor made so much money he decided to go back into business for himself.

Mom's home in Livermore, where the Kaiser operation was located, was a large tent with flaps on the sides to roll up in good weather. Don slept at one end of the living room, Louise at the other end. The kitchen and a bedroom were built across the back. R.G. and Evelyn slept in the bedroom with Rich in a crib.

That left no place for a washing machine. Mom put it on a concrete porch out back inside walls of canvas stretched around to give some protection from the weather. She would heat the water on her wood stove and carry it to the washing machine, pour it over her clothing, and run the cylinders for a time. Afterward she used a hose to rinse them and then ran them through a pair of rubber rollers to squeeze out the water.

Mom saw to it that her children went to church, regardless of the inconvenience. When Kaiser sent them to live in Eureka, farther north in California than Mom had ever lived, she learned about three girls holding meetings in the Eureka Baptist Church. She took her family to hear them and became acquainted with "The Duff Sisters." One of them, Helen Duff Baugh, later started the Christian Women's Club in Kansas City.

Helen, Evangeline, and Olive presented their program that night—all single girls with a heart for evangelism. Helen was twenty-one, Evangeline nineteen, and Olive seventeen. The girls were having a hard time finding a suitable place to stay where they could be together. So Mom rented an apartment big enough to house the girls, herself, and her children while Pop finished his job for Kaiser, ten miles away.

"We had beds all over," Mom remembers. "My mother was with us. She would cook lunch for the men out on the job, and I'd cook breakfast and dinner at the apartment. Louise slept in the parlor with the Duff girls and Grandma America; Don and the girls' brother were bunked on the back porch. R.G. and I slept under the stairway next to a window on a mattress placed on the floor. Rich slept on a crib mattress beside us."

The Duff Sisters and R.G. finished their respective commitments at about the same time, so they all went to Stockton and continued bunking together in the LeTourneau house while the girls held meetings in that city. When the girls left to attend The Bible Institute of Los Angeles, R.G. and Evelyn, on the spur of the moment, had a creative thought: why not enroll with them and sample the curriculum of Bible school? R.G.'s sisters, Sarah and Marie, living in Upland, California, offered to take care of the children while their parents matriculated in the downtown Los Angeles Bible school.

R.G. had quit school at the age of fourteen because he considered himself "a man growed," and Evelyn had been married before finishing high school. Their return to school at the ages of twenty-six and thirty-eight was a bit traumatic. R.G. lasted for ninety days. When Henry Kaiser called and offered him a construction job in the desert, he closed his books and left. Mom picked up her youngsters in Upland and drove back to Stockton.

When the time drew near in 1929 for her fifth child

to be delivered, a fruit farmer, for whom her husband was leveling land, offered the LeTourneaus an acre of Kadota figs if Mom would name her new son "Samuel." Evelyn had been pestered in grade school by a kid named Sam Stern and had grown to detest the name.

"I'll not do it," she declared when R.G. pressed her for a decision. She later weakened and allowed that Roy could have the middle name of Samuel. It wasn't enough. The offer was withdrawn, and the Le-Tourneaus never got the fig trees.

Did Mom ever see her indomitable husband depressed?

"Yes, of course. There were times when he was low in spirit, but he always bounced back," she reflected, remembering one time in particular. One fall in the late 1920s, he came home one day and sank into a chair, discouraged. R.G. tried to get jobs working sandy ground in the winter time and adobe soil in the summer. Winter's moisture made the adobe impossible to maneuver with his tractor and graders.

"The job in the sand is finished," he announced, "and I've got nothing else for the whole winter. I don't know what we're going to do. Guess I'll pull the equipment into the shed and store it till spring."

After breakfast the next day he put on his hat and breezed out the door. "I'll tune up the tractor's engine and bring 'er into the barn," he called back.

But while he was working on his tractor, a rancher strolled up with a proposition. "Say," he began, "I've got an orchard over here that I want pulled out so I can plant grapes. How about it?"

R.G. shook his head. "I'm not interested in a little one-day job. I need one that will last all winter at five bucks an hour."

The rancher pressed him, so he relented. "It'll cost you ten dollars an hour," R.G. warned, trying to get rid of him.

"OK," the rancher agreed.

"It'll cost you from the time I leave here until I get your job done," R.G. added.

The rancher consented to the price. "Go to it."

Other ranchers passed the orchard and saw what was happening. This led from one job to the next at ten dollars per hour all winter, as the entire valley, it seemed, was switching from fruit trees to the more lucrative vineyards.

R.G. worked steadily, not losing any time moving around all winter at ten dollars an hour instead of the five dollars for which he had prayed so hard.

CHAPTER SEVEN

TWO IF BY AIR

MOM was never handicapped by indecision. She had packed and moved twenty times from 1917 to 1935, and when opportunity knocked she didn't complain about the noise; she was ready to pack again.

Officials of the Caterpillar Tractor Company, whose dealers were buying LeTourneau scrapers and fitting them onto their machines, met in a smoke-filled room far away in Peoria, Illinois, and brought to a vote an executive decision, which the secretary was directed to send to R.G. LeTourneau in Stockton, California.

> If you would build a plant back here where the steel is processed, we wouldn't have to ship it to California for you to build your graders and have you ship the graders back to us again for fitting onto our tractors.

Several days later Mom and Pop were on the Santa Fe's "Super Chief" threading through the Rockies, then streaking over the plains toward the pioneer city on the Illinois River. Peoria's youthful days were marked by entertainment; LeTourneau would help turn it into a city of industry.

From their room at the Jefferson Hotel, both set out on their appointed rounds—Pop to meet the men in the smoke-filled room and to find a building site, Mom to buy or rent a house big enough for eight LeTourneaus (seven, actually, since Don was enrolled at John Brown University High School in Siloam Springs, Arkansas). Pop found his site first—a level bit of acreage on South Adams Street where he would build the plant that would yield undreamed-of fortune for his budding company. He later split with Caterpillar over a disagreement about his two-wheeled tractor called the "Tournapull." Caterpillar later had to capitulate and admit LeTourneau had a golden idea. Today the machine is moving dirt all over the world.

Before returning home to Stockton, Mom rented a house at 501 West Armstrong Street, a semifashionable three-story brick structure on a wide street lined with mature trees. Mom put two cribs in the dressing room, gave Louise a room of her own, and then passed the word to the factory that workers without a place to stay could board with the boss's family.

Soon the youthful workers, hungry for a job in the middle of the Great Depression, began streaming into Peoria. Up to thirty men at a time boarded in the LeTourneau house. They paid twelve dollars for their weekly food and a bed.

The LeTourneaus could not find a Christian and Missionary Alliance Church in the vicinity, so they settled for a small Missionary Church in the low-rent district of Peoria's south side. Mom and her charges filled about half the church, because word soon spread in the plant that whoever went along with the LeTourneaus to church was automatically invited to their home for Sunday lunch.

Establishing the homestead in Peoria, to hear Mom tell it, was as routine as an eight-to-five job. A girl named Catherine Boyle had come alongside in Stockton to feed, wash, and manage the five children left at home. Mom phoned home and told her family about the house, setting the date for their big move to the Midwest. When she arrived home, all the talk was on moving to Peoria as quickly as possible.

Pop and his crews had loaded the machines on flatcars and were already in Peoria when his family boarded the Sante Fe "Super Chief" for their ride into a new life.

It was summer when their east-bound sleeper, hissing steam, eased out of Stockton Station. Picking up speed, it dived with a roar beneath the overpasses toward Arizona, to the delight of the youngsters onboard, snaked across the Southwest, then over the Midwest plains, finally transporting them to their new home.

At mealtimes, passengers disembarked and ate at the Harvey House Restaurants along the main line. Louise, Rich, Roy and Ted managed fine, but Mom had to feed one-year-old Ben. By the time she had him satisfied there was no time for her to eat.

A porter came to her rescue. "Mrs. LeTourneau," he suggested, "the next time the train stops, you run around to the five and dime and pick up a spoon, a dish, and a cup for each of you. Then you have the restaurant pack up your food, and you bring it back here on the train. I'll set up a table, and you'll get to eat."

R.G. met the train at 5:00 A.M. in Chillicothe, Illinois, because the train didn't go through Peoria. His youngsters were all dressed up for the reunion.

"Welcome to Peoria!" Pop boomed as he met his family at the depot.

Who, watching the arrival of the LeTourneau children that morning at dawn, could have realized the impact on Peoria that single family would make. Millions of people would one day hear the testimony of the man from Peoria . . . would marvel that a Christian would give 90 percent of his earnings to God . . . would enroll in Mom LeTourneau's camps . . . would hear the gospel at the "Tournata" compound in Liberia and throughout the land of Peru, where LeTourneau's machines based at "Tournavista" would build roads and carve farmland out of jungle.

In that first morning, each member of the family did what might be expected: Pop went back to the factory; Mom went to the store for food; the children explored the house and laid squatters' claims to their favorite rooms.

The grocer might never have seen a grocery list as long as the one Mom laid on his counter. He might also never have seen a thirty-four-year-old customer pass out and sink to the floor, but he knew what to do when it happened. He filled a small bucket with water and poured it on her face. When Mom came to, she felt as though a wave had hit on a sandy California beach.

"Where am I?" she asked meekly.

"You fainted," the grocer exclaimed. "Dead away. You just sank right to the floor, so I threw cold water in your face. Is anything wrong?"

Mom sat on the floor chuckling as she wiped her face dry. "No," she replied, "I'm just plain tuckered out."

The grocer rushed to get a chair in which Mom sat to recite her list as the storekeeper filled the order.

"Now then, I'm going to drive you home," he declared.

"I'm all right now," Mom replied. "There's no need. . . ."

"Not on your life. I'm going to drive you home and that's that."

The grocer kept his promise, but what grocer in 1935 wouldn't have? It was the best kind of public relations, and Mom traded at that store for many years, her lists growing longer as her house filled up with boarders.

Not many people would want all those paying guests in their house day after relentless day. God had given Mom LeTourneau a special love for boys. To her it was a ministry; some fellow-Christians couldn't understand why Mrs. LeTourneau would surround herself with all those young men.

The wife of a LeTourneau factory worker, who also was a member of the church they attended, decided she would do the same. She opened her house to boarders, but her husband objected to her "running around." The woman had invited some of the boys to her house when her husband was out of town.

"Evelyn's doing it," she declared. "Why can't I?"

But her husband insisted, and the dormitory ended.

How did the family like having the roomers around?

"Didn't bother me," say Rich and Roy. "Louise was the only one who had a hard time. Imagine being teased constantly by fifteen or twenty young fellows."

When Mom's sister, Fdna, came to Peoria to visit, she always went back to California with funny episodes to relate about her transplanted relatives.

"I'd go with her to deliver stew to the workers at the plant and Evelyn would drive right down the trolley tracks, which were level with the pavement, to keep the stew pot from spilling," Edna recalls, laughing.

"When we went shopping for groceries, it looked to me as though Evelyn had bought the whole cow. She carried it to the car. I got in my side and waited, but Evelyn had disappeared. I got out, walked back to the trunk, and spotted her in a ditch, the meat on top of her. As she had opened the door, her feet started to slide in the snow. Her shoes took her to the bottom of the ditch."

Edna recalled the time when Mom picked up a preacher at the Peoria depot. "She drove so fast and hit so many bumps that one time she threw her arm in front of the preacher to hold him in place. She had become so accustomed to holding her children in their seats that without thinking she did the same for this man of the cloth."

She remembered an episode ten years earlier when Evelyn, loading supplies in Stockton to haul to her husband who was building a road near Boulder City, Nevada, encountered a lawyer who asked for a ride out to the building site to discuss a matter with R. G.

"Sure, you can ride along," Evelyn told him.

The lawyer sat in the back, his fingers clenching the seat and his knuckles growing white as Mom sped over the winding dirt roads.

"They're working right down there," she called above the noise of the engine as she turned over the crest of a hill.

"Y . . . you're not going to *drive* down there, surely!" the lawyer shouted.

"Why not?" Mom shouted back as she nosed the car straight down into the embankment, touched the brake pedal lightly, and slid to the bottom on top of a small avalanche of stones, rocks, and dirt.

"That lawyer was scared spitless," says Edna.

Mom liked to save on heat bills and would turn her Peoria thermostat down so low at night that frost would appear inside on the window panes. Edna always enjoyed hearing her sister call upstairs in the morning, "Ted! Ben! Do you have your snowsuits on?"

Stories of life at the big house abound: Roy's scarlet fever, a running anxiety about Don and his youthful imprudence, complaints from neighbors about too much noise at the big house, Louise's loneliness as the only girl among a houseful of "cat skinners," and lively conversation at the board.

When Pop became carried away telling a story, Mom would look at him with pretended scorn. "Oh, Pop, you're exaggerating!"

"No, I'm not," he would reply, "I'm just blowing it up a little so you can see it better."

In those first years some men shared a bed—one rising at night for the graveyard shift, the other falling into it exhausted from the day shift. But they were employed. Happy days had come. The WPA and the CCC and Roosevelt's bold policies had brought hope to the Great Plains—hope as big and as wide as the machinery those workers were building down at the plant.

On April 1, 1936, Mom bought a carton of Oreo cookies. She carefully scraped the sweetened white goodness out and put shaving cream in its place. These she put up into a cupboard, leaving the door slightly open so they could be seen. The good ones she placed on the table for her boarders to enjoy as treats, but she knew what would happen.

As the thundering herd swarmed into the house they were on guard. April Fool's Day—what would Mom have up her sleeve?

"These any good?" one asked, eyeing the plate.

"Sure they're good," Mom replied.

"What's those up there in the cupboard?"

"Now, you just leave those alone. You eat the ones on the table."

The boys looked at each other. "We want those cookies in the cupboard," they decided.

"We fussed around and I wrestled with them pretty good. I could hold my own in those days. We fussed and I wrestled for quite a while until I finally gave in and let them at the cookies in the cupboard. They all made a grab and stuck 'em in their mouths, then they come up a-spittin'. 'Well,' I said, 'I *told* you to eat the ones on the table.'"

That evening another shift came in for supper, after which the cook set the polluted cookies on the table. Pop Cook was the first to put a cookie into his mouth.

Immediately he tasted the shaving cream, but he just kept chewing as the others watched him. When he swallowed, the younger workers all grabbed the cookies and took bites. They began to gag and fuss and sputter and jump around the room, dramatically protesting their culinary fate. Pop Cook told Mom later, "I was blowing bubbles all night."

One Sunday morning as her car was filling up with passengers, she invited the two girls who helped her in the kitchen to pile into the back and sit on the laps of the men. As the car started down the road toward church, Mom happened to glance into the rear view mirror and noticed that Elmer Strein had his hands in the air.

"How are you doing back there, Elmer?" Mom asked.

"OK, but I don't know what to do with my hands," he replied.

Elmer had been raised by an invalid mother. He never dated and was socially quite gauche. He eventually married one of Mom's cooks who was some twenty years his senior.

Life was not always smooth in the big house full of boarders. Next door to the LeTourneaus lived a tightly knit Jewish family that didn't always appreciate the antics of the LeTourneaus and their guests.

One episode particularly disrupted the serene neighborhood. Mom had just finished serving breakfast to the night-shift workers. She had purchased a thirty-dozen crate of eggs which was sitting on the breakfast table. One of the workers grabbed an egg and let it fly at one of the girls waiting table. The waitress got her hands in front of her face in time, but the raw egg caught the edge of her glasses, splattered, and ran down all over her clothing. The men howled with laughter and the girl, able to enter into the fun, managed to laugh with them as she wiped off the sticky mess. The laughter and hysterics could be heard up and down the street.

The discontent of the neighbors continued for another year until Mom found another "dormitory" on Glen Oak Boulevard.

"Evelyn had the patience to work with those kids when other people would not have," Edna observes. "She put up with their nonsense. She was never perplexed, always concerned about people."

When one of her boys got drunk and stayed out late, Mom applied the "coals of fire" treatment. She would fix an especially nice breakfast and serve the man in bed. Many a convicted man would rather have been slapped than to be treated to such hospitality.

"God loves you," she would remind him. "We want you to get up and eat your breakfast."

The domesticated evangelist had a nearly perfect success rate among her roomers. Some made professions of faith in the home, others in the little Missionary Church, still others in special evangelistic meetings that Pop arranged at the plant.

Mom loved them all. There is no clearly defined line between her services to the family and to her roomers. Detractors say she was gone too much; her children, except for Louise, look back on the extended family as more fun than inconvenience. Like their dad, the five boys relished the thunder, sparks, and hot grease of the factory from which machinery would magically appear.

By 1937 Mom and Pop LeTourneau were familiar figures in churches, luncheons, and rallies where the newly famous industrialist was asked to speak. The LeTourneaus always paid their own way and often left an offering of their own for the host organization.

Great crowds would gather at the airstrips to see the LeTourneaus' plane arrive, for in the late 1930s, travel by air was reserved for the very rich or for officials upon an important mission.

Airplanes have played a big part in Mom's life. She prefers to travel by air, feeling safer than on the ground. The first pilot to work for the LeTourneaus was not instrument rated. He got caught in a canyon one day and couldn't get out. Pop quickly calculated the distances on his map.

"Make these turns," he told the fledgling pilot, "and you should be right over our destination."

And sure enough, the layman's math worked perfectly.

The family of planes included the following: a Waco five-place, single-engine aircraft (1939); a seven-place Northrup low-wing craft (1940); a Lockheed #12, seven-place twin-engine (1941); a Lockheed Lodestar seating 12 (1943); and three war surplus A-26 bombers built by Douglas Aircraft Company—the fastest plane of World War II. Their pilot, Royce Barnwall, had more hours in the single-seat cockpit of the A-26 than any other pilot in history. "Barney" used to say before takeoff with R.G., "Well, I'll check the weather, but I know we're going to fly anyway."

The LeTourneau family's preference for air travel was strengthened by an unexpected event on a lonely highway north of Murfreesboro, Tennessee. Aside from the new Chevrolet that Mom purchased when they moved to Peoria (taking the train to Detroit and driving the car home to get a good deal), she later kept the family in LaSalles, Buicks, and larger cars for more room and greater protection.

Bob Jones College in Cleveland, Tennessee, invited Pop and his male quartet, composed of workers in his factory, to speak and sing at the school's 1937 graduation ceremonies. In one of those big Buicks Mom, Pop, and the quartet started on the long trip but never got there. On Route 41 in Tennessee, the driver of an oncoming car turned to look at the passengers in the rear of his car and veered into the path of the LeTourneaus' sedan.

Pete Rutschman was driving; Pop was snoozing in the back seat between Orin Rutschman and Bill Eitzen. Mom had just traded places and was sitting in front with Pete and Norm Dirks. Pete yanked the wheel hard to the right when he saw the car coming toward them, but the cars collided. An explosion of dust and flying metal punctured the quiet countryside, leaving mangled bodies, death, and injury in the stillness that followed.

All three occupants were dead in the car that had rammed the LeTourneaus' Buick. Pete had been killed instantly; so had his brother Orin sitting directly behind him. Mom was knocked unconscious and suffered deep gashes in her legs. Both of Pop's legs and his pelvic bone were broken. His hips were pushed out of their sockets, but he remained conscious. He whispered hoarsely to Bill Eitzen, "If Mom and I don't make it, I don't care what happens to the money, but use any of it you can get your hands on to be sure our children are taken care of . . . that they come to know the Lord."

Mom remained unconscious all through the loading onto the ambulance and the short drive to Rutherford Hospital in nearby Murfreesboro. The car was junked and the commencement address undelivered. Mom regained consciousness that evening and from her bed began making arrangements to get home. At the end of the week the injured went home by two private ambulances under the care of a nurse named Sarah, whom they hired and who lived with the LeTourneaus throughout their recuperation and for two years afterward. She later married Bill Plunket, one of Mom's boys.

In 1939, when Adolph Hitler was stirring up evil, Mom was stirring up good. She "packaged" carloads of Peoria youth and transported them to camps. This small beginning was the start of a new career that would lead many to righteousness.

CHAPTER EIGHT

GOD'S KINGDOM FOR A CAMP

IT had all started in 1932 when Mom LeTourneau hitched a flatbed trailer to a Model T Ford and hauled a gaggle of giggling teenagers to Mount Hermon in the Santa Cruz Mountains of California. Camping, she discovered, was an efficient way to focus a young person's mind on eternal issues and lead the most unresponsive young person to spiritual regeneration.

In a camp her youngest brother had turned his life toward heaven; at camp she saw her husband's hardest employees clean up their lives and sanctify their families by making commitments to Jesus Christ. At camp she had seen troubled boys transitioned from the street to school or to gainful employment and release from crime.

Now she was filling up cars again in the Great Plains, caravanning to the northwest corner of Iowa, near the Minnesota state line, in Arnold's Park nearly five hundred miles from Peoria. Why so far?

R.R. Brown, pastor of the Omaha Gospel Tabernacle, had invited R.G. to address his congregation, and there Mom learned about Camp Okoboji. For a week at a time she rented a house, and for three years Mom loaded her big LaSalle with noisy youth and led a stream of cars to the open spaces of the former Indian campground.

In 1937, following the shattering accident that took the lives of two employees and crippled her husband, Mom had at her disposal dividends from company stock after her husband established the LeTourneau Foundation and transferred to it 90 percent of the company's resources for God. She quite naturally began to look around for a campsite to buy.

Winona Lake, Indiana, the home of Billy Sunday, was an evangelical mecca in those days. People from cities and counties throughout the Midwest rented cabins, lounged on the sandy beach, or picnicked on grassy shores beside the beautiful blue lake. The Winona Lake Christian Assembly had built the huge Billy Sunday Tabernacle to which the most prominent speakers of the day were invited—including R.G. LeTourneau.

While Pop thundered from the pulpit, Mom inspected the grounds. On the southern part of the assembly she found and purchased Bethany Camp, a beautiful lakefront property of five acres with a large house, cottages for campers, sports equipment, rowboats, canoes, a pier, and sprawling green lawns for team sports. The camp was served by the nearby Warsaw, Indiana, airport where the LeTourneau plane could shorten the trip from Peoria to an hour.

Students like Hank Pucek would come from Wheaton College, a hundred miles to the northwest, to direct Mom's summer recreation program and to counsel the campers. One of her earliest speakers was thin, wiry Wheaton graduate Billy Graham. Mom suggested to the directors of the Winona Lake Christian Assembly that they might like to schedule him also, but they at first declined.

"He's only got three sermons," they pointed out. "We've heard them."

Another ally in Mom's camping project who had considerable influence, deep spirituality, and good connections was V. Raymond Edman, president of Wheaton College. Dr. Edman, a former missionary to South America with the Christian and Missionary Alliance Church, was named to the board of the Le-Tourneau Foundation. He put on overalls to help clean the cabins, haul out the winter debris, cut the grass, and paint the buildings in preparation for a new crop of summer youth.

At Bethany, Mom's daughter Louise met Gus Dick, a Fletcher College student from Iowa, whom she would later marry. At Winona Lake, crossroads of summer evangelical outreach in the Midwest, Mom spent many a moonlit evening at a rustic table on the lawn talking with a troubled camper, or leading one of them to Christ, or dealing with an errant employee.

In all of her patient outreach to other young people, Mom's heart was heavy for her son Don. A photograph taken at the end of his sophomore year of high school in 1938 shows a tall, strong lad with a shock of dark hair above alert, keen eyes. Would her son ever find the footsteps of his parents or yield to the Spirit of God?

In 1939, during her first year at Bethany, the rumblings of change were upon her. It came to bless the family in a most unlikely way.

CHAPTER NINE

MOM'S MARCH TO GEORGIA

MOM extended hospitality one evening to Dr. Richard A. Forrest, founder and president of the Toccoa Falls Bible Institute in northeast Georgia. At one point in the meal he told the LeTourneaus of his mission: a round-the-world trip to visit alumni of the institute.

"I know I'm going to meet many needs as I travel," he told his hosts. "I wonder if you would care to provide some funds just to help the most needy of the students I'll meet."

R.G. did not hesitate. He drew two thousand dollars (half the price of a small farm in 1938) from the Le-Tourneau Foundation and placed it in his guest's palm with a hearty handshake and a "Godspeed."

When Dr. Forrest returned, he sent R.G. a detailed account showing how every penny of the gift had been spent. Pop was so impressed that he offered to build a plant in Toccoa near the school to give the students work, if Dr. Forrest could find a suitable site.

Mom shared with Dr. Forrest her burden about her eldest son.

"You send him down to us," he said. "We'll take care of your son."

The man was good to his word on both accounts. He found a splendid piece of flatland served by a railroad and also "took care" of Don LeTourneau as only a man gifted in dealing with young people would know how. He sent regular reports of Don's activities on campus; he noted how well the strong lad could work; he encouraged them to keep praying as Don drew nearer and nearer to the end of his term.

Suddenly it was time to uproot the home in Peoria and move to the South. In the seven hundred mile move to Toccoa there is no mention of the work, the details, the emotion that must have been involved in the transfer. Mom had done it before; a new challenge suited Evelyn Peterson LeTourneau. Railroads would carry the heavy equipment for the new factory, and trucks would carry her household belongings; but she would "march" to Georgia by car, her children lined up in her big sedan.

Pop was asking his wife to move into a community of steel dormitories that he had welded together on a knoll in the grimy shadow of an industrial site at the end of a runway.

One of the articles in Evelyn's advice to young mothers is, "Never argue in front of the children; go with your mate behind closed doors if you must disagree." She would have occasion to follow her own advice in Georgia.

Late in 1940 Mom decided that it was time to build her own house. Since her husband had designed a special 4-by-8-foot metal prefabricated panel for houses, she agreed that their next house would be made of steel. R.G. and his famous steel house had appeared in Bob Ripley's "Believe It or Not" newspaper column when R.G. floated one of them across the Illinois River at Peoria. The four-inch-thick double panel walls were made of 12 gauge steel one-tenth of an inch thick, embossed with a pattern to give them strength. The space between the two panels was packed with vermiculite as insulation.

"The prefabricated houses were pleasant enough," practical Mom recalls, "but I wanted closets in them. Pop, however, could see no reason why I wanted closets in each bedroom. To him they were 'just a lot of extra expense.' He had bought metal cabinets that you could hang clothes in. They each had two doors and were quite functional when put into place. He installed these in each of the dormitory rooms where we were living. 'Those are just good enough for anybody,' he decided."

Mom had equally decided that she didn't want those cabinets in the bedrooms for clothes closets. The two bickered about the matter for days, Mom resorting to crying and R.G. storming off to the plant in disgust.

One day the woman diffused her anger in the biblical way: she gave it up. She made her appeal one more time at lunch. Then after her husband returned to the office she sat down at her desk and wrote a note:

Let's not argue anymore about the closets. We can just stay where we are. It isn't worth arguing and getting upset. Let's forget it. I love you anyway.

She took it to the office and slipped it unnoticed on R.G.'s desk. By midafternoon the head draftsman was at her door. "I don't know what come over Pop," he said, shaking his head. "He came in and told me to bring these blueprints over to you right away and tell you to fix them any way you wanted to."

As she spread the blueprints before her, Mom smiled and pondered the matter. There were never long stretches of romantic interludes in her life, but adjustments were made as she went along and settled at the point of tension. It is easy to imagine the smiles around dinner that night, the light conversation, and the warm feelings around the heart. It would seem surprising if R.G. went back to the factory that night and worked until ten o'clock as he did every night of his life except Sunday, but he probably did.

A picturesque pine tree stood on the site where Mom wanted to build her house. Pop sent the bulldozers to level the land. She knew those Caterpillar tractor operators pretty well and the power of that machinery. She knew that her tree could come down with a nick of that blade in a few seconds of carelessness. So as long as the Cat worked around that tree, she stood in front of it, daring the driver to go near her prize.

"I didn't want to build a house around a tree that was all skinned up," she said.

All this occurred in the autumn of 1939 when the

boys were getting settled in school and the factory was rising steadily on the land near the Toccoa Falls Institute.

Life in a steel house suited the practical Le-Tourneaus. It had five bedrooms, two baths, and cost six thousand dollars to build. They had to drill a hole to hang a picture and put up with snapping and cracking sounds as the steel contracted by night and expanded by day. The children had rooms of their own and quickly felt at home in the deep South.

"We moved there in the fall of 1939," son Roy recalls, "and finished out that year in the city school. Since we had just moved in from Illinois, that made us Yankees and put us in a bad position. We wound up in quite a few fights, even though we tried to explain that we were Californians, not Yankees."

Louise was nineteen and engaged to Gus Dick by now, Don was eighteen and Rich fifteen—both enrolled in the Toccoa Falls Institute boarding school nearby. Roy was ten, Ted seven, and Ben five—all still at home.

Even then, youthful traits forecast future careers: Louise, the homemaker; Rich, the fastidious record-keeping scholar; Roy, the persuasive salesman, singer, and preacher; Ted, collector of wires, motors, radios, and anything that would run; Ben, the neat, tidy boy who had a place for everything—including his money, which he managed to possess longer than any of his brothers.

The year 1940 was one of the most eventful of all for the LeTourneaus, bringing both joy and sadness to the family. On Valentine's Day, Louise was married to Gus by Dr. Forrest at the First Presbyterian Church.

At the wedding reception in the Albemarle Hotel, a man from the lobby staggered into the reception drunk. The uninvited guest took it upon himself to show the photographer how to get Louise's gown just right for the picture, but instead he tipped over one of the baskets of flowers and it doused her bridal dress and train in water from her knees down.

Later, as Louise bent over to cut the cake, her veil fell forward and was ignited by one of the candles. She calmly reached up, pulled it off, and handed it to one of the girls attending, and kept on cutting the cake.

Observing the scenario was a medical doctor named Schaeffer. Ten months later he would be performing an appendectomy on Evelyn LeTourneau. The only one of the family he would trust to be with him in the operating room was Louise. He explained, "Anybody who went through fire and water like you did at your wedding and stayed calm, I'll trust to stay with me in the operating room."

In Toccoa, the LeTourneaus received regular reports from Dr. Forrest on the progress of their son Don. No joy equaled the report from Don himself when he phoned across town the message for which they had waited so long: "Mom, Pop, I've been saved."

Don had other news to report as well. At eighteen, he had fallen in love again, this time with Wilma Morris, twenty-one, and had proposed marriage. (At sixteen he had made an abortive attempt to marry a California girl he had met at Mount Hermon.) Don and Wilma were united in May at the end of the cap-and-gown high school graduation service of Toccoa Falls

Institute, with the entire student body and faculty present as their guests.

The happy couple moved into one of the five steel houses and became involved in the LeTourneau manufacturing empire. Don's first assignment was the building of a power press to form steel sheets for building purposes. He had it finished when a call came from a road building crew in North Carolina requesting a part to replace one that was broken. Don, having learned to pilot a small aircraft, volunteered to fly the replacement to the site and land on the newly built roadbed.

Plant manager Jack Salvador looked toward the north. "Remember, Don," he warned, "if you see black weather up ahead, don't get into that stuff."

Don called Wilma. "I'll be back by the time you have to go to work at the cafeteria," he said. "Come and go with me."

One of the night-shift workers overheard. "Listen," the young man objected, "Wilma gets to go with you everywhere. I've never gone once. How about it? Let me go this time."

Don relented and Wilma was relieved, fearing she wouldn't get back in time to punch in at the LeTourneau dining room. The boys climbed into the small, yellow single-engine plane. It was August 19, 1940. Don had been married for three months. The little plane climbed on course and disappeared in the black clouds. The turbulence that Salvador had feared overcame the small craft. It was torn apart in the air, and both young passengers were killed.

Mom still weeps at the memory of that day. Pop kept

the sorrow in his heart through the funeral and the burial. When he went into the shop after the funeral and turned on the press that Don had built, it worked perfectly. Only then did he break down and sob for the son he had lost.

Friends donated money for a special fund that was used to build an auditorium at Canandaigua Lake in upstate New York. It still stands as the Don LeTourneau Memorial Auditorium.

"It's hard to understand it all yet," Mom reflects, "but someday I know we will, since there were eight or ten boys saved through Don's death during a week of meetings at the school."

A mother is softened by such experiences. Mom's influence was keen at the plant. She served as confidante to the fellows enrolled in LeTourneau's Machinists School, often sitting outside in her car to counsel the boys who needed a mom. When one was finished, she would honk the car horn and out would come the next in line.

She was also an unregistered nurse at the plant. She took in a boy hurt in a motorcycle accident . . . another who had the mumps . . . still others who took sick with influenza and other diseases.

Her boys' wishes were her commands. One afternoon the students/workers at the machinists school wanted to go frogging down at the lake.

"Will you cook 'em if we bring you some frog legs?" they asked Mom.

"Sure. I'll cook all you bring home."

Off they went a-gigging, but instead of bringing

home the expected dozen or two, they returned with 186 frog legs stuck to their gigs.

As Mom prepared to undertake the cooking, she recalled her sister Edna's first experience with frog legs. She had put them in a skillet to fry and then turned to other tasks in the kitchen. Soon her screams brought her husband running. The legs were leaping out of the pan all over the kitchen. Mom made certain she had a lid on the operation that evening. It took her until midnight to cook all those frog legs.

Mom's first illness occurred in Georgia on Christmas Eve, 1940. She had spent the day rushing about, gathering food for the maid's pots. Toward the end of the day she complained of a pain in the area of the appendix. She phoned the only doctor she trusted and found that he had joined the Army. However, he was at that moment en route home to spend Christmas Day with his family.

Instead, he spent Christmas Eve removing the appendix of Evelyn LeTourneau while their families gathered-to celebrate the birth of Christ.

A hysterectomy in 1953, cataract surgery on both eyes in 1971 and 1974, and the installation of plastic knee sockets in 1975 sum up her medical history.

Mom was instrumental in building a new radio station with the call letters WRLC in Toccoa and hired Virgil Craig to operate it. The original call letters, which stood for "Robert LeTourneau Company," were later changed to WLET to reflect a growing use of the LET symbol in the company.

As LeTourneau built his Georgia plant, he bulldozed

a dam across the creek that ran in back of the plant. The large body of water that developed was named "Lake Louise" after their daughter. A road ran across the dam where R.G. had leveled the ground and designed and built a large steel building. It looked from the air like the hub and spokes of a giant wheel. In the center, or hub, he had a large domed meeting hall. Leading out from this were five one-story buildings. One "spoke" was omitted to serve as an entrance to the center building. As might be expected, Mom sponsored young people's camps there in the summer months. In later years the camp was sold to the Southern Baptists.

Mom saw in her camps a splendid outreach to the men her husband hired to supervise his manufacturing plants. With the company plane at her disposal, she regularly took contingents of fifteen or twenty men and their wives to Bethany Camp in Winona Lake, Indiana, where they would hear the gospel of Jesus Christ. Many point to those trips as life-changing experiences.

There was always time for fun. Those top-management representatives from the LeTourneau plants often had not traveled far from home. A flight to a northern city was an experience they would treasure for a lifetime.

One morning Mom roused her friends in time to catch the 5:00 A.M. limited from Warsaw, Indiana, to Chicago, a hundred miles away. When they boarded the train, most of the travelers were asleep. In those days, only a generation ago in time but a light year away in terms of civil rights, whites were uncomfortable in the same quarters as "colored." Just as Mom was settled for the journey she heard a voice at her elbow.

"Mom, I know you don't mind. Would you change places with me?" The man pointed to his seat, which was shared by a black man. Mom gladly changed seats.

The windy city was abuzz with morning commuters when the party disembarked. Mom steered them into a restaurant at the train depot where the men ordered "grits."

Their waitress frowned. "What's *that?*"

"Same as that right there," one of the Southerners answered, pointing to a neighboring table.

"Oh, that's cream of wheat," she replied.

"What's *that?*" he inquired.

From the top deck of a double-decker bus she pointed out the sights of the city. Most of them missed the impressive Marshall Field department store because they were looking for an airport. She took them to a Chinese restaurant for a special treat, reserving a room all to themselves.

"Mom," they said, "we don't know how to order this stuff. You order for us."

So she assembled a suitable menu, ordered for twenty people, asked the blessing, and started to eat. When she looked up no one was eating. They were watching her. One man poked at his plate of food with a fork. "I'll declare," he murmured, "that thing moved."

"Come on, eat," she chided. "This is delicious."

"Not me," declared one, then another. They watched their hostess, then sneaked out for a hamburger afterward. She had them on the train and back to Winona Lake that evening in time for the gospel meeting.

The trips to Winona Lake seemed to grow longer as the years passed. After her husband established a plant in Texas in 1946, Mom decided to cut the trip by more than half by selling Bethany and purchasing Pine Lake twelve miles south of Little Rock, Arkansas. Built as a country club, Pine Lake featured a golf course, a lake, one large rock building at the edge of the lake, three wooden houses, a chicken house, a barn, and sheds on a total spread of two hundred acres. She hired a caretaker and a crew and sought to make Pine Lake a home for troubled boys and give them an opportunity to hear the message of Jesus Christ.

During the Christmas holidays of 1947, carloads of plant employees and her own children helped to rake the grounds, clean and repair the buildings, and get them ready for camp activities.

The Pine Lake community never fully supported the camp. School authorities would not allow Mom's disadvantaged boys to enroll in their classrooms. Neighbors resented the presence of outsiders. Soon after a big Christmas dinner in 1947 Mom decided that the venture would not succeed. She sold the camp and purchased the East Texas Boys Ranch in Lindale to carry out her programs.

CHAPTER TEN

TAMALE PIE FOR SEVEN THOUSAND GUESTS

MARY Evelyn LeTourneau knew that something was going on in that restless head of her mate. This man she had selected from Stockton could create monsters to peel back the earth's crust or clear a jungle but couldn't find the clothes closet in his own house (he was there only to wash, eat, and sleep). So word might have been passed to her brood even before Pop announced that they might be expected to unhook themselves from the society of Georgia and move to a new factory site.

"I need water transportation," Pop complained in his land-locked office at Toccoa, "to move my products in and out. And I need men—lots of men."

If there was a flicker of disappointment in Mom's countenance, it didn't show. Pop did not read her face. Either his was directed toward the plate of food in front of him or it was absorbed in a set of drafting sketches for something new, something bigger, something to drive the salesmen crazy by interrupting the assembly

85

line and making an adaptation that would hold up orders and anger customers.

The two had not been coupled for the sake of tranquil rest; so Pop, at fifty-five years of age, flew off to Vicksburg, Mississippi, to look at land beside Old Man River himself where he would build a third enterprise. Mom sighed, put the children in the care of a motherly woman, and hooked a house trailer to her Buick for a trip west.

"Come on, Wilma," she said to her daughter-in-law. "We might as well go see what those men are up to."

She found them crawling like worms on the seats of Caterpillar tractors, damming up a creek, and pounding together small wooden houses on a hillside with wooden flaps instead of window panes. Oh, the price men pay in lack of creature comforts to put smokestacks into the sky and broad sheet-metal roofs over spinning lathes and assembly-line chains.

Mom and Wilma drove as far into the scene as they could until the Mississippi mud claimed them. With help from the stronger sex they got their trailer situated on level ground and called it home. The men bathed in their new lake and drank water from a half-inch pipe hastily strung from a remote well.

It is said that a man must build a house, have a son, and plant a tree during his earthly sojourn. In the LeTourneau family it was the "weaker" gender that did all three. Before she gave up such activity Mom had five sons, planted innumerable trees, and built four houses.

Another house by Evelyn would now rise on the levee

by Ol' Miss, right in the middle of World War II. She picked the ground, sketched her plans, and took them to the county board or whatever they called the office in Mississippi for official approval.

The young credentialed agent took one look at the plans and shook his head. "Mrs. LeTourneau," he said, "don't you know there's a war on? You can't build this house. There's just no way. . . ."

"Well, who's the head man for this area?" Mom interrupted without showing emotion.

"Oh, he's in Atlanta, Georgia," she was told in a manner that could be construed as condescension. What woman of forty-two would take the trouble to journey all the way to that far-off city at a time of scarcity such as World War II had brought to the country? Little he must have imagined that Mom was soon sitting in her favorite seat aboard Pop's Lockheed Lodestar flying toward Georgia with the blueprints in her purse.

After a night's rest in Toccoa, she drove into Atlanta ninety miles away with her plans. As happened often, the status of celebrity followed her and kept her from moving as rapidly along with a project as she would have liked.

"Are you the wife of R.G. LeTourneau?" the official asked.

"Yes, I am."

"Well, I know your husband," the man beamed. "He spoke in our church. Wonderful man. . . ." Now, what could he do for his visitor?

Mom presented her house plans, which by now

showed signs of usage that gave evidence that she had been holding them close over not a few miles in search of the elusive stamp of approval.

"You can't build the house as you have it there," he said. But then he warmed to his scheme. "I'll tell you what to do. You put in the plumbing for this bathroom here, but just leave it below the floor and make that front bathroom a clothes closet. And leave the carport off for right now and build it in two sections as two small houses. You can join them later after they're finished."

He pointed out that a surveyor's marker would have to remain exposed for sighting at any time the officials wished.

Stamped. Approved. Legal.

Just to be prepared in case a knock on the door some day would bring a surveyor looking for a strange sort of stake pounded into the ground under her house, Mom had the concrete slab poured, leaving a protective hole so one could lift the carpeting, raise the cap, and peer into the hole to read the official marking. But no knock ever came.

Finding a building contractor in those years of scarcity was nearly an impossibility. She managed to coax a cement mason into pouring the slab and then into laying the blocks. Mom guided him all the while with chalk to indicate where she fancied her windows would come according to the official plans.

The steps leading up to her front door were a project Mom tackled by herself. With shovel in hand she cut the "shelves" of dirt, laid in the concrete blocks, and trowled in the mortar. A photographer snapped her picture and sent it to editor Tom Olson, who put together the company paper *Now*, sent free to anyone who requested it. When that issue was delivered to the subscribers, letters poured in objecting to the president's wife wearing a pair of men's overalls. In reply, Mom wrote a paragraph in the next issue asking what the readers thought would be more proper than a pair of overalls for bending over on a windy day on a hillside to shovel dirt and lay block. She never received any suggestions.

Now established in Mississippi, the three children still at home gathered around her once again. (Louise was married; Rich, at nineteen, was representing the company in Australia and later joined the U.S. Army Engineers in the Pacific.) Mom did none of the things her peers might have expected. She visited no antique guilds, she shunned expensive clothing, she joined no women's clubs or society rosters. The one "exclusive" dress she was talked into buying she later saw on the back of a corpulent cleaning woman in New York City. She never again bought an "exclusive" anything. The only charge account she ever opened was negotiated to establish credit so she could return some merchandise. She only charged for convenience, believing strongly that no one should charge anything unless they had the cash to pay for the goods purchased.

Mom did like to have fun with her sons. Occasionally one of them would get a "date" for her among his high-school chums for a night out, since Pop was married to his drafting table and at work every night.

"We always had more fun with Mom along," Roy remembers.

Everybody in Vicksburg knew about the LeTourneau plant rising in the Mississippi mud out on the levee. Each Saturday the crews of workmen were highly visible on downtown streets visiting the places of amusement. Mom would drive up to the gate and load her station wagon full of men, then head for town. Astonished bystanders would marvel as twelve . . . fourteen . . . up to fifteen men emerged from the station wagon.

Mom also transported crews of men to church on Sunday mornings. Some undoubtedly were "biscuit Baptists" who went along for the restaurant meal en route home, others out of Christian duty, some to gather with fellow-saints for worship.

On one particular Sunday the woman who owned their favorite restaurant came out to apologize. Waitresses had quit, and there were not enough people to serve the customers. She and her husband were doing all the cooking in the back.

Mom pulled on an apron and began carrying food to the customers and clearing the tables. When the poor woman found out who her customer was, she developed something akin to the catatonic state, her hand frozen on the cash register, her mouth agape, her eyes wide.

A similar event happened soon afterward when the company division heads invited city and state officials to a dinner on the plant site. Mom corraled some girls to wait tables, but all were too shy to serve the head table, so Mom took it. Throughout the meal, one of the more gregarious types at the head table pretended to be dissatisfied with the service, the food, and the table decorations. He teased Mom because she knew how to give it right back.

After the meal was over and introductions were made, Mom was called out of the kitchen to acknowledge the applause. When that man at the head table saw that he had been teasing Mrs. R.G. LeTourneau, he sank down under the table out of sight and actually sat on the floor, holding his head.

"Why didn't someone tell me?" he whimpered to the delight of his colleagues.

When one of the machinists became ill with appendicitis, Mom drove him to the hospital and stayed until after the operation.

"You must be one of the top brass out there at the plant," the doctor commented to the patient.

"Nope," said George Thompson. "I'm just a machinist apprentice."

Pop enjoyed the gathering of Vicksburg officials and grew expansive in his suggestion that the plant throw open its doors in the summer of 1943 to invite the entire city for a special dedication.

"Mom, I want you to make a tamale pie."

"For the whole town?"

"Yep."

"How many do you think there will be?"

"Oh, I'd say seven or eight thousand people."

"Pop, I don't have a tamale pie recipe for eight thousand."

"Sure you do. Your recipe calls for eight. Just multiply it by one thousand."

"But what would I cook it in?"

"You leave that to me," he said, pulled on his hat, and left for work.

At the plant, Pop selected a large sheet of steel and rounded it at the bottom so that it resembled a deep trough. He bent a lip six inches wide on the top sides, then welded metal on each end. Next came a framework upon which the kettle could rest, holding it two and a half feet off the floor where a log fire would burn to heat the tamale pie. Wooden benches alongside the kettle allowed four boys with scrubbed garden hoes to stir the tomatoes, hamburger, corn meal mush, chili, and other ingredients for their guests.

Meanwhile, Mom was at the Piggly Wiggly Market on Washington Street with a grocery list unlike any the workers had ever seen. With a straight face she stepped up to the meat counter and ordered. "Two thousand pounds of hamburger, please." The meat cutter looked so shocked, Mom had to laugh. She spent a few minutes trying to convince the young man that she really wanted a ton of meat, and she had to have it in a week.

She wrote to her sister Edna in California for immediate shipment of a case of Grandma's chili powder. She bought four new garden hoes, scrubbed them good, and assigned four boys to walk beside the kettle and stir the concoction. She first mopped the sides of the pot with shortening, browned the meat, then added tomatoes, corn, chile, cornmeal mush, and three one-hundred-pound sacks of onions that had to be chopped by hand in "a crying good time."

When the giant tamale pie was cooked, R.G. hoisted the trough with a crane onto a framework built on a chassis with rubber tires. This was hooked to a tractor and pulled through the center aisle of chairs. Eight girls on each side served more than seven thousand people in about forty-five minutes.

There was enough and to spare. The big kettle was lifted by a crane and set outside. After a couple of days, a hog farmer asked for the leftover pie to feed his swine. Before Mom was in bed that night, he phoned from his farm out of town frantically reporting that his hogs had eaten her tamale pie and were "all dying . . . just going down like flies."

"There's nothing I can do now," Mom told him, "but phone me in the morning. I'll see if I can get a vet out there."

In the morning the farmer's voice was calm, and Mom could tell the crisis had passed.

"What happened?" she asked.

"Well, that cornmeal must have fermented and made my pigs drunk. They just slept if off, and this morning they're fine."

At Vicksburg, Pop had a tractor plow up a plot of ground where the LeTourneaus lived, twelve miles out in the country. Mom would get his breakfast at seven each morning, then go down to the garden and pick beans or wash cucumbers and load her car with whatever was in season. Afterward she would return to the house and get her youngsters off to school.

As a surprise for their children, Mom and Pop had one of their factory workers bulldoze a huge hole on the property for a swimming pool. Ted and Ben had learned to swim at Lake Louise back in Georgia by putting their fingers into the handles of empty gallon jugs, and anticipated many hours of fun in their own pool.

However, just after the hole was dug, Mom read about the drowning of a boy in the family pool. She ordered the tractor back, filled up the hole, and planted grass there instead.

It was best to live without regret.

CHAPTER ELEVEN

THE SCHOOL THAT KNACK BUILT

S TRAIGHT west, across the state of Louisiana from Vicksburg, Mississippi, lay the east Texas town of Longview. In 1945, R.G.'s antenna had caught the vibrations of large deposits of steel ore and a new steel mill lying just north of Longview. He needed new sources of steel, so he would have a look.

"This time I'm going along," Mom announced. "If you're going to build another plant in Longview (she knew he would), I want to keep it out of the mud."

Like her husband, Mary Evelyn had learned to think big. But there was no virtue, she reasoned, in working knee-deep in silt, no matter how reasonable the price of the land.

The plane had been serviced and checked. She climbed into her seat beside Pop, and before she could become hungry for lunch they were landing in Longview to pick up selected city officials. The late November trees had become bare, and the chill of winter was in the air already.

Newspaperman Carl Estes, owner of the *Longview News & Journal*, climbed in first, sat down across from the LeTourneaus, and started going over the route they would take. The plan was to fly north, circle Daingerfield where the steel mill was located, have a look at the terrain, then drive up later by car to negotiate purchases of the precious metal.

Watching that plane thunder down the runway brings to mind the far-reaching implications of the smallest turn of the wheel of providence. Watch as the pilot turns the flying machine, banking slowly northward. Had he not turned at that precise moment the plane's orbit would not have allowed the following conversation and the beautiful campus of LeTourneau College might never had been built.

"What are those?" asked Mom, pointing down to neat white barracks stretched out like a quilt on one hundred and fifty acres of land.

"Oh, that's Harmon General Hospital," Carl Estes replied. "They've just closed it and they're dismantling it . . . gonna ship everything out."

"Seems to me if somebody could get to the right person in Washington, they could get that for a school and not just tear it down," Mom reflected.

Estes whirled around and faced her. "Will you put a school there if I can get it for you?"

Mom glanced at Pop. He gave his familiar "sic 'em" nod, and went back to his reading of *Iron Age* magazine.

"Yes, I would," she replied.

Such is the confidence of people who have both the

will to work and the resources with which to carry out their programs.

In Mom's mind she imagined only a bigger and better machinists school, like the one organized in Toccoa and later moved to Vicksburg, that could prepare workers for the new Longview plant. She saw also another congregation of boys to disciple and to bring into the kingdom of God. Like the woman of Proverbs 31, "she considereth a field and buyeth it."

The red tape in Washington started to roll through the machinery of government. In early December Mom walked those grounds to inspect the deserted compounds. The ground was quite level, rimmed with tall trees, only 125 miles east of Dallas on well traveled Highway 80.

On February 1, 1946, government officials handed her the ceremonial keys in a special service inside a large building that was a gymnasium. Three months from the time she first saw it from the window of the plane, Evelyn LeTourneau had a school. On her lap was a book of inventory ten inches thick, listing items she could buy at ten cents on the dollar. Imagine the cards and letters from friends when news of LeTourneau Technical Institute got into the company publication, *Now*—expressions of support, wonder, and skepticism about what the president's wife was getting into now.

Nearby on Mobberly Avenue, Pop was bulldozing land to build his fourth manufacturing plant.

Mom commandeered a couple of young men who had come from Vicksburg to help with the new plant.

She selected the first building on the northwest corner, took a deep breath, and started in. When she turned the key and opened the first door, she found a building piled to the roof with skeins of yarn in every color imaginable. In other buildings she found crutches and wheelchairs and linens and bedpans. In still others she found four-burner electric stoves, which she bought for ten and twelve dollars each, later to sell them to married students enrolling in LeTourneau Tech.

"We had to leave all the buildings as they stood for ten years," Mom explained, "in case the government needed them again."

One would be used for a snack shop, others for dormitories, administration and office buildings, and classrooms.

Pop invented a special mold the size of a house into which he could pour cement. He would then lift the outside mold with a special U-shaped machine, deposit it on a concrete slab, unbolt the outer mold and . . . Presto!—a concrete house. Several of these houses are still in use near the plant in Longview and in Vicksburg. The shell needed only the addition of window and door casements, and a coat of sealer to keep out moisture.

By late March, Mom had worked her way through the entire medical facility. On April 1, 1946, the school was dedicated; classes began the next day. The lady with only a year and a half of high school training herself was now the prime mover in an educational institution that her knack for organization had built, hand in hand with the heavenly resources of providence.

Resourceful Mom let nothing go to waste, including

a large refrigerator with four big drawers built to store dead bodies, which the hospital had used as a holding tank for cadavers. Since Mom was involved in building and expanding her Bethany Camp at Winona Lake, she shipped the body cooler to Indiana and replaced corpses with fruit and vegetables in its labyrinthian shelves. The staff eyed the monster suspiciously, but her family still laughs heartily at the memory.

The government required that Mom accept for enrollment GIs returning from World War II.

"Many of these boys were hard to handle," she recalls. "They thought that anything belonging to the Army they were entitled to. At night they would remove exhaust fans, locks, racks, and anything that suited their fancy, take them downtown, and hock them. Others would walk down the corridors punching holes in the sheetrock. Some would come onto the campus drunk, and we were not slack in disciplining them."

A snatch of her message at a chapel service shows how she handled the matter: "Remember, I may not know whether you're drunk or not, but your buddies will, and they won't have any respect for you if you get up and leave now . . . if you won't face up to it."

She called each offender into her office, talked to him straight, prayed with him, and encouraged him to do better.

"We got a lot of them straightened out," she says. "Of course, there was a lot of them that we didn't, too."

Two men were brought from the Toccoa plant to teach the boys, but both died within the first year. She hired Allen Tyler from Peoria to move to Longview and run the school. In those days not many Christians were qualified to teach a group of budding mechanics, but gradually the picture changed until today, the full faculty of more than sixty men and women have all made commitments of faith. As word got out, letters like this one began filtering in:

> I can teach welding (or machine shop or mathematics), and I'm getting sick and tired of the public schools where you can't talk to the boys, you can't witness to them about Christ, and you can't even give your testimony. I'd take less money if I could teach in your Christian school.

Mom selected a long, two-story campus building as her house. She had the stairs at each end taken down and a stairway added in the middle—eight bedrooms upstairs and a living room, dining room, kitchen, and laundry on the first floor. Somebody wanted to see the blueprints, but the only "blueprints" available were in Mom's head. The place was called "The Big House" and served as the LeTourneau home for fourteen years.

Niece Joyce Farnham came from California to start a student center on campus and to operate a canteen. One of the married students commented to her one evening, "Every time I come here I get in the doghouse."

"That's it," Joyce exclaimed. "We'll call it 'The Dog House.'" The name stuck until the R.G. LeTourneau Memorial Student Center was built and the old Dog House was dismantled.

The school name was changed in 1960 to LeTourneau College. It has become the only private Christian coeducational college in the world that in one school offers engineering, technology, special technician programs, flight training, the arts and sciences, teacher education, a strong Bible program, and missionary technology. In 1970 the college earned full accreditation, granted by the Southern Association of Colleges.

Thousands of alumni and all the current student body know the little lady in the duplex at the edge of campus on Evelyn Drive as "Mom." For many years Mom stayed in the canteen until the place closed—talking to the boys about school, counseling those with problems, then packing them into her car and transporting them in cold weather to their various dormitories.

Michael Patrick, an Indiana farm boy, was one of the young returning soldiers who was talked by his family into enrolling at LeTourneau. Tall and handsome, Mike was quickly spotted by Mom and as quickly tagged as a suitor for her niece Joyce.

"I had a brand new Studebaker," Mike said, "and of course all the guys wanted to borrow it. But when I didn't have wheels, Mom was always there to take me wherever I wanted to go. I found myself invited into the LeTourneau home for dinner, intimidated completely by the company of these famous people. I remember the day when I saw this beautiful, slim, California niece of Mrs. LeTourneau walk across the platform at chapel in this school of men and I found my heart in my mouth. I remember, too, being invited to the Le-Tourneaus to enjoy their company—and to meet Joyce. I remember nights when Mom would counsel with me in her car—even holding my hand—and gradually I came to see that I really did have a chance with Joyce, who later became my wife."

Mike and Joyce moved to California where Mike worked in the Caterpillar dealership of Mom's brother Howard for some years until he stepped out in a leadership capacity with Campus Crusade for Christ.

By now Ted and Ben were the only ones at home. Richard was married, Roy at Wheaton Academy. Mrs. Hildier Jensen (Richard's mother-in-law) was in the LeTourneau home to clean, cook for the boys, and keep the home fires burning. Mom was a kind of "chaplain-at-large" on the campus, enjoying the opportunities to know her students and to turn their hearts and minds toward those things that she considered most important in a Christian education.

CHAPTER TWELVE

HALLELUJAH! I'M TIRED

MOM has a salty common sense. Another woman might have considered any one of her undertakings an entire career, or something to appear on a radio talk-show about, or perhaps even to use as the subject of a book. None of these occurred to the woman behind the LeTourneau activities. Driving across the country, sketching plans for a new house, cooking for an army of hungry workers, flying across the Atlantic Ocean in an Army surplus bomber or taking the family jet to Peru, purchasing and operating youth camps, or founding a college—these occurrences were taken in stride and not thought to be extraordinary.

Now that the college was humming smoothly, Mom could fly occasionally with Pop on his weekly rounds. He went to the Peoria plant on Friday, to a youth rally somewhere on Saturday, to a speaking engagement in a church on Sunday, to Toccoa on Monday, to Vicksburg on Tuesday, and home to Longview on Tuesday evening. On Friday of that week the weary rounds would be resumed.

When R.G. would get into his Volkswagen "beetle," which he said drove "just like a car," to travel from the campus Big House to his office across the road, he could scarcely keep his mind on his driving. Several times he was hit on the busy thoroughfare. Mom took the signal. She designed and built a sprawling ranch-style house next to the plant, so he could come and go in a golf cart on the western side of the street without having to wend his way through streams of traffic. It seemed to fall her lot always to live in the smoky shadow of a rumbling mill.

You can take the girl off the farm, but you can't take the farm out of the girl. With Ted and Ben married in 1953, and the nest emptied, Mom found she could give more time to her East Texas Boys Ranch forty miles from Longview in Lindale, Texas. Stocking it with prized Charolais cattle became her special delight. Once she located several Charolais cows for sale in up-state New York and flew up in the company plane to have a look. She paid five thousand dollars each for two cows in this herd.

In Harlingen, Texas, she tried to convince a reluctant rancher to part with a calf.

"How would you get it to Longview?" he asked.

"Well, I could take it in the plane," Mom replied.

The rancher sized her up. "Yes," he concluded, "I believe you would."

The East Texas Boys Ranch began accepting boys from broken homes, juvenile detention centers, law-

104

yers' offices, police stations, and frustrated families no longer able to cope with an errant offspring. Mom never met a boy she couldn't handle. "If I punished a boy who was guilty, he took it," she says. "But if I tried to punish a boy who was not guilty, he would fight like a tiger."

As she drove into the ranch and parked one afternoon, a swarm of boys clustered around her car. She opened the door and sat with them a spell, asking questions and carrying on light banter. One of the boys handed out a sassy, depreciating remark. Like lightning, Mom's hand shot out and slapped him so hard in the face he was knocked down.

"Listen," she said, "I don't take that kind of talk from my sons, and I'm not going to take that kind of talk from you."

Word spread quickly that "Mom really packs a wallop."

"A child who never gets corrected," she explained, "thinks nobody cares about him."

She was often at the ranch for morning milking and one day heard one of the boys griping because they had to get up so early to tend the herd.

"Well, I milked cows when I was younger than you are," she told the complainer.

"Oh, pooh," he replied, "you never milked a cow in your life."

"I did too. My dad had a dairy and I milked six cows every morning. Get me a pail and I'll show you."

Mom was able to milk fast enough to keep a head of foam in the pail, but she told friends later she was glad they didn't ask her to milk a second cow because her arms were aching so badly she could hardly finish the first.

Mom had a peach orchard at Lindale, and when her boys didn't behave, she broke off a switch and applied the punishment. One little boy, a bit younger than most, had been sent to the ranch because his mother found him incorrigible. After he had spent a month there he wrote home a glowing report: "I'm getting along fine, and I guess I will as long as Mom's peach trees last, and she sure has a lot of them."

She was in Battle Creek, Michigan, one day while she was on a trip with Pop and wanted to get her blood pressure checked. She had gained weight steadily through the years and weighed 180 pounds. Her blood pressure rose right along with her weight.

No doubt the physician noted Mom's strong shoulders and arms because he began to reminisce about growing up on a farm.

"I used to milk cows," Mom said.

"Well, I can tell if you've ever milked one," the doctor responded.

"Go ahead," Mom replied.

"OK. What kind of a stool do you sit on when you milk?"

"A one-legged stool."

"Correct. What do you do with the cow's tail when she tries to switch it around your neck?"

"You tuck it under your knee."

"What do you do when the cow tries to put her foot in your bucket?"

"You stick your head into her flank."

"You've milked, all right," the doctor decided.

Walter Knowles, a Montana butcher and lay preacher, was managing well as the director of the East Texas Boys Ranch, treating Mom's young charges with tough love. But in 1949 her nephew Dick LeTourneau needed a chaplain for the Toccoa plant; so Mom surrendered her prized employee. A LeTourneau truck was leaving Longview in an hour and a half. It was all Walt needed to pack his earthly belongings and hitch a ride to his new life. After the Toccoa plant was sold, Walt managed the Lake Louise Hotel and Conference Grounds. Later he went to Liberia where he helped Louise and Gus in developing the experimental missionary station called "Tournata" (recounted later in this book).

Walt's position at the East Texas Boys Ranch was not easily filled. Men came and quit quite regularly. If a man had love in his heart for the underprivileged boys, he didn't have the discipline to keep them in line. If he was skillful in discipline, he lacked the love to go with it.

One applicant seemed to be perfectly suited. Mom introduced him to her charges, and he started out with a big splash. But one night shortly after was his last. It was after midnight when the man phoned Mom with a touch of panic in his voice.

"Mom, get a police officer quick and come out here to the ranch. These boys are trying to *kill* me."

"What?" she gasped, coming fully awake. She glanced at the clock: 2:00 A.M.

"They've got knives out of the kitchen, and they're after me with those butcher knives."

107

"Well, where are you now?"

"I'm in my house, and I've got all the doors and windows locked. Hurry. Get the police. Don't come out here alone."

"OK, hold steady," she said. "I'll be right out."

She sighed and dressed wearily, warmed up her car, and drove to the ranch alone. She pulled in alongside the dormitory so her headlights would shine in through the windows. Everything was dark. There wasn't a sound.

Mom opened the door and stepped inside. Still not a sound. Motionless forms lay under blankets. She flicked on the light. Instantly every blanket was thrown back and every body popped up, fully dressed.

"What happened here?" she demanded.

"Aw, Mom," they said, "he's scared of his shadow. We was just teasing him."

Mom gave them "a good talking to" and ordered them back to bed and to sleep. "I don't want to hear any more of this at all."

She waited to enforce her command, then left. The director would have to be dismissed; he had lost the respect of his boys who responded only to strong authority and love that would not let them carry out their whims. Mom's health was failing. She had to act quickly.

Mom appealed to the Baptist orphanage in Dallas, visited facilities in Austin and in San Antonio, and finally found a place for her boys in an institution near San Antonio. In 1957 all the boys moved either to San Antonio or home to their parents. It was the end of an era. Her camps were now a part of history.

In an issue of *The Word, Work and World,* published by the Christian and Missionary Alliance Church, A. B. Simpson told about a thirteen-year-old Sudanese Christian girl who was ordered to carry a heavy burden on her head for three days with hardly any time for rest. The girl became pitifully weary. As a Christian believer, however, she refused to complain. She thought that she must continually be praising the Lord, no matter how tired she was. Finally she could take the load no farther. She sat down, discouraged, and burst into tears. "Hallelujah!" she wailed. "I'm tired."

Mom had carried her loads for more than four decades. It was time for a change.

CHAPTER THIRTEEN

NATIONAL MOTHER OF THE YEAR

S UNDOWN is a time for anniversaries, milestones, the gathering of friends to remember, the constant thumbing of photo albums, the fondling and redistribution of accumulated items, the visits from grandchildren, and the laughter with friends as old stories and jokes are resurrected and embellished with undiminished glee.

On August 29, 1967, Mom and Pop reached their fiftieth wedding anniversary. Three thousand messages of good cheer engulfed them. Representatives from the various manufacturing plants attended the party. A Liberian co-worker and his wife came from Tournata. A grandson was given special leave from West Point. And the day was properly commemorated with a huge, decorated cake. No mention was made of the elopement so long ago, for the *Capilla de Casamiento* in Tijuana had been long forgotten.

Another bright milestone, which illuminated for a moment the lengthening shadows of their lives, was Pop's eightieth birthday two years later. The men in

Peoria who had worked closest with R.G. journeyed down with a huge plaque fashioned like a car. An artist had painted a cartoon character unmistakenly R.G. and the text read: "You made the Tournapull, the Tournascraper, the Tournalathe, and now you turna eighty."

Mom's anniversary cake for R.G. required two weeks to prepare. She baked the layers using two quarter-round tins made especially for this purpose—four for each inch-and-a-half layer. Each piece was kept in a freezer until the anniversary date when the entire cake was assembled. Mom used ninety-six cake mixes and built the cake twelve layers high. The finished product measured thirty inches in diameter with a hole in the middle. Hadn't Pop taught her to think big? The boys at the plant made her an electric motor out of stereofoam, which they painted LeTourneau yellow and placed in the middle of the cake.

Before the frosting went on, she sat the cake on the dining room table and threw a towel over it. She knew her husband would not bother to ask what was under the cloth or even look at it.

As they were eating their dinner she glanced over at the cake just in time to see half of it slide onto the floor. The cardboard supports had not been able to hold it up. Pop good-naturedly helped her to put it back together in time to celebrate.

From then on her man's "spells" began to come more frequently. In Chicago, Richard and Roy noticed during a speech that his words were slurred. Occasionally an arm would refuse to move as Pop sat at his drawing board. The spasm of a blood clot inside his head was the culprit, medical analysis revealed.

Despite his weakening condition, Mom persuaded him to make a trip to California in the spring of 1969 to visit the LeTourneau and Peterson clans. In Howard's home, Pop suffered a particularly bad seizure and spent a week in a San Francisco Bay Area hospital. They traveled home in the company plane when R.G. was feeling better.

As she rifled her stack of accumulated mail back home, Mom trashed a few form letters and advertising brochures and read quickly a letter from the American Mothers Association, which had announced that she had been selected by a special committee and was to be named 1969 "Texas Mother of the Year."

"I didn't think much about it," she recollects. "I gave it to Nels Sjernstrom and asked him to answer it and thank them for the honor." She had little time to think about those things while taking care of her "Mr. R.G.," as she liked to call him later in life.

The American Mothers Association warmly invited Mom to the agency's national convention in Los Angeles late that spring as a representative of Texas. Since Pop had recovered well and was urging her to go, she decided to try it. Roy and Shirley flew Mom to Los Angeles where she was met by her sister Edna and daughter Louise. They reserved rooms next to each other in the convention hotel.

On the second morning an early phone call from Dorothy Lewis, president of the American Mothers Association, brought her quickly awake.

"Are you alone?" Mrs. Lewis asked in a low voice.

"Yes."

"I must see you right away. I'll be right up."

Mom dressed, made a quick call to the nurse in Texas to make certain Pop was resting well, and was ready when Mrs. Lewis tapped lightly on her door.

"Still alone?" she whispered as she tiptoed inside. "Evelyn, you've been chosen as the National Mother of the Year."

"What. . . . I can't imagine such a thing," Mom replied.

"Now you can't tell anybody, not a soul, not your sister or your daughter or *anybody*. It will be announced at the banquet two days away."

As soon as Mrs. Lewis left, Mom decided to take a walk to calm herself down. *Imagine,* she fussed, *having to keep still about such news for two days!* She was afraid the news would slip out if she spoke with her sister and daughter. But they guessed as soon as the speaker started her coy little remarks leading up to the grand surprise. Amid the convention's applause Mom walked to the platform and was introduced. Lawrence Welk popped in from behind the curtains and posed for pictures with the "National Mother of the Year." That night Mom and her family joined the convention at a Los Angeles club where Lawrence Welk and his orchestra were playing. Again she joined Lawrence Welk on the platform—this time to dance, but she had to tell the disappointed musician that she did not know how.

Then came more stops around town for photographs with celebrities and movie stars and more anxious phone calls to Texas to inquire of the nurses, "How's Pop?"

NATIONAL MOTHER OF THE YEAR

R.G. became excited when he learned that Mom was coming home and seemed to understand when the nurses told him she had been named National Mother of the Year. He insisted on going to the airport to meet her.

The LeTourneau jet finally sat down on the Longview runway amid the cheers of half the city, the music of the high school band, and the official welcome of the Longview brass. People grabbed her and hugged her, and she tried to be sociable, but her mind was on Pop. She wrenched away finally, and hurried to the car. But he had suffered a massive stroke sitting there in the car and never spoke or responded again. Four weeks later he went to be with the Lord.

In her days of mourning, Mom imagined Pop at rest in heaven, discoursing with the One he had served so faithfully, perhaps embracing their tiny son Caleb who had missed his chance to know his father in this life, greeting their beloved Don, and yes, maybe her father Oscar as well.

In the letters toward the end of July that year came an invitation from a woman's club in San Antonio inviting her to speak at a special gathering.

"Here, Nels, write them and tell them thank you, but I can't do it."

Her trusted friend disobeyed. Nels wrote back, thanked the group, and accepted. When Mom received a letter of confirmation she phoned across campus. "Nels, you rascal. You know I can't get up there in front of a crowd and talk!"

"Oh, yes you can," he replied. "I'll help you with your speech."

Nels flew with Mom to San Antonio. Smartly dressed young men in red jackets rolled out a red carpet for her when she arrived on the plane. A girl handed her an armful of red roses.

"I was petrified," she says, reflecting back on the event. "Then when I stepped inside and saw that mass of women I nearly died. I don't mind talking to a bunch of men, but when you get up in front of women they're looking to see what you have on, how your hair is fixed, and what jewelry you're wearing."

Suddenly the woman at the microphone was finished with the introduction and Mom, Mother of the Year, clutched the speech Nels had carefully helped her prepare and aimed herself at the podium.

"I consider it a great privilege to meet with you on this particular occasion as a representative of all of the mothers in this country. I hope that I can share something with you that will have lasting value and that may help us as mothers to be more effective in our everyday living and in the management of our family life."

Then she looked out at the crowd, lost her place in the text, and decided that instead of reading her speech, she would "just share some things" with her audience out of her experience.

When she sat down, fighting tears, she shot a whisper to Nels who was sitting on the platform. "I'll *never* do this again."

"Oh, yes you will," he replied smugly. And she feared he meant it.

Christmas at home that year was the first in fifty years without Pop at the festive table. She heard in memory his booming voice, saw him savor his favorite

116

dishes, responding to the grandchildren's tugs on his sleeve.

Grandpa had been a man in motion, not the doting type with listening time for the next generation. If you caught him at noon in his office, you could ride home with him for lunch on his golf cart, jiggling and bouncing along, listening to him sing or tell a joke. Grandma was the one who posted your photograph on her bulletin board, who remembered your birthday, and whose cookie jar was seldom empty.

During the Christmas season, Nels Sjernstrom was quietly working up his next assignment. The 1970 New Year's Day Tournament of Roses in Pasadena, California, set as its theme that year "Holidays around the World." The City of Alhambra, California, designed a float featuring Mother's Day, and who better to ride on it than the National Mother of the Year?

"She'll be there," he wrote.

The rules were simple: Be on Orange Grove Boulevard at the start of the parade at 6:30 A.M. Wear a long, yellow dress with long sleeves with no wrap except a little fur cape.

Mom slipped into thermal underwear, knowing that mornings in California can be frigid. She was carried to her seat on the float, which was built with tiers of flowers and covered with a canopy. Mom was surrounded by roses, carnations, and baby orchids.

Every inch of the float had to be covered with flowers or by some part of the flower's stalk. "Mother's Day" took the top theme prize as Mom rode down Colorado Boulevard on the dazzling creation, waving to people on both sides of the street—more than a million of them who had come to watch as they have done for all of the ninety-five years of this nationally televised extravaganza.

Roy was there to meet her at the end of the five-and-a-half mile parade. As they lifted her off the float with a forklift, Roy grabbed her. "I don't want to smile again for a week," she whispered. "My face hurts."

Before Mom's knees got so bad that she couldn't walk without help, she had spoken in cities from coast to coast and in Canada. The jet was sold, and she moved into a large duplex that she designed on a street named for her next to the college. Letters lacking the "Evelyn Drive" address found her, however. An African in Liberia addressed his letter simply: "Mom, Longview, Texas," and it came promptly to her door.

Except for a special occasion, Mom's last speaking engagement was in 1979, but through her singular honor as National Mother of the Year, her influence was broad and continues even today.

CHAPTER FOURTEEN

"DEAR MOMS"

In a typical message to mothers, Mom LeTourneau shared the following ponderables about life in the home.

IT takes more than a house to make a home. Today I live in a house that is a modest house, but a very nice one. During the fifty-two years of our married life I have lived in twenty other houses, but all were homes. I do not look back upon any of them with a feeling of dissatisfaction.

In the early days of our marriage we lived in a farmhouse with just a pump at the kitchen sink. I have lived in tents over considerable periods of time because I would go with my husband in construction work and settle wherever he was working. In many cases I'd cook also for several men who worked for him.

We slept in a tent, and I cooked out in the open. For a bathroom we would stretch a canvas around three or four trees.

I have lived in cement houses. I have lived in houses

made of steel, wood, and stucco. I have also spent considerable time in what they call a cookwagon. It was about nine-by-twenty feet. We slept in one end with two children and cooked and ate in the other end. There was no gas or electricity—just a cookstove. We had only kerosene lamps. Water came from a nearby spring. I fed five men working on that job. I know what it is to live without any of the modern facilities that we have today.

Those who did not arrive on the scene early enough to bathe your children or take a bath yourself in a galvanized tub in front of a kitchen stove have really missed something. But throughout all of those years with what would appear to be great trials, I can honestly say that because of the relationship that existed between my husband and myself and the relationship with our children, we knew what it was to have a happy home.

I felt that it was not merely my *duty* as a wife, but rather my *privilege* to contribute to the success that my husband was making in life. How well I remember those early days when he was just getting started in his business. In order that he would not have to take time off from work to get supplies, I would often take the car and the two small children to town to pick up steel rods, welding materials, or other things that could be placed in a rack on the side of the car or inside, and then I would bring them back to him. Really, those were exciting days.

One reason that I can look back upon those days without a tinge of regret or feeling that those were hardships is that my husband was so happy in his work.

Some basic principles need to be remembered by young people who are entering into early homemaking.

I suppose there's nothing that people seek more than happiness. However, there is a great deal of misunderstanding about this topic. I often present recipes from my kitchen in our monthly publication, *Now*. Of course, when you give a recipe to anyone, you have to tell them all of the ingredients that go into a particular cake, pie, or whatever it happens to be. So, if we talk about happiness, we need to consider the ingredients that go into happiness. Some people don't like the word *happiness*. They think it isn't deep in its meaning. They say that happiness is dependent on what happens. This means that if what happens isn't pleasing, they don't believe they can be happy. I say that happiness is possible regardless of what happens.

During fifty-two years of our marriage I was not free from sorrow, losses, and problems, but two things that never changed have made it possible at this point to write in big letters over all of those years, "Happiness."

The Bible tells us over and over again that God loves us. When we believe this, it is impossible for any circumstances of life to rob us of our happiness. In trials we learn to know and experience the peace of God that passes understanding. Romans 8:28 promises: "All things work together for good to them that love God, to them who are called according to his purpose."

The second thing that assures happiness at all times is love for each other. This is more than a sentimental attraction. It is a respect and appreciation that grows from year to year; therefore, every trial and testing deepens the feeling of our need for each other. How I

121

wish I could get across to young couples the joy of commitment to God, the blessedness of reading God's Word together, and the unity and strength that come through prayer together. This is a recipe that never fails.

I want to emphasize an area of life and experience that needs much attention—the Christian family's devotional life. How sad it is when homes are established without giving Christ his proper place. Every girl should be helped to develop her own devotional life at an early age. Her effectiveness as a Christian mother is related to her nearness to the Lord. If every family would make the Word of God and prayer a daily experience, there would be fewer broken homes.

An old saying reminds us, "Those who pray together stay together." This is certainly true. It seems quite clear that we, in our generation, have the responsibility and privilege of demonstrating how fellowship with Christ brings happiness, and in that way we will teach our daughters to be good Christian mothers.

Have you as a Christian ever been in a situation that made you wonder if some Christian practices were appropriate?

One evening in our house we had a rather large dinner party. We were entertaining a group from a Chamber of Commerce who were there to encourage Mr. LeTourneau to come to their city to open a new factory. Dinner had been served, and as everyone settled back for that extra cup of coffee, our youngest son, who was then ten years old, got up and walked away but soon returned with the family Bible. He handed it to his father and sat down. I will confess, I might have been tempted to let our devotions slip by that night, but we couldn't when our young son expected us to have them. "A little child shall lead them."

My husband took the Bible, explaining to the guests that our custom was to read a portion of Scripture and pray. This seemed very natural to all of our family; but what seemed strange and surprised me a little bit was that so many of the guests commented about it. Of course they said it was nice to see it, but it seemed that they were a little surprised that anyone had family devotions anymore. They noticed, too, that to the ten-year-old boy it was the most natural thing to do because it was always a part of the family dinner.

The Word of God says that we should not conform to this world, but be transformed. That's in Romans 12:2. One translation reads: "Don't let the world squeeze you into its mold."

As Christians we need to remember that it is always appropriate to let our light shine before men, and it is most effective when it can be clearly seen that this is the normal and natural way of life—not something that was just put on for the occasion.

I would like to emphasize the importance of consistent discipline—not after a child is five or six years old, but from the first. No one likes a spoiled child. We do our children a grave injustice by spoiling them. We must be consistent in what we say. Don't let them do something several times, then when our nerves are on edge spank them for doing the same thing. A child wants and needs correction. It makes him feel secure and loved. Give firm orders, then follow up in love. Always go back and talk to the child and pray with him after correction.

Most young people who are giving trouble today are confused and insecure because they have not had discipline in the home. I had a boys ranch for delinquent teenagers. Nearly all of the teenagers told me their parents did not care for them because they never corrected them. The parents either let them do as they pleased, or they beat them for everything. Either extreme is bad. They need correction with love. Sometimes it is hard to stick to what we say. It's better not to say anything than to give an order and not follow up on it.

The home has a tremendous influence upon a child as he is growing up. We may read the Bible in our homes, pray in our homes, and entertain guests hospitably. We may tithe and give generously of our money. But all may be weakened if there is constant criticism of the church or of the members or of the pastor and program of the church.

It's pretty easy to get caught in this because we are all so human. Some of us don't have children at home anymore, but I want to take every opportunity to encourage young couples who are establishing homes to make them the best centers of influence they possibly can. Consider the effect upon young people who are growing up if they hear a great deal of criticism in the home. Take a tip: make your home a place where criticism is seldom heard but where praise is a common thing.

Someone may ask, Do you mean that you shouldn't have a mind of your own? That you should always go along with everybody? No, I don't mean that. But when it is necessary to disagree or make a criticism, it should be done in a spirit of love.

Life has taught me that it is more common for us to blame than to praise. If we are going to make a mistake in going too far in one direction, let's keep it on the praise side.

If we are frequently criticizing our church, school, teachers, and community leaders, how can we expect our children to have respect for their superiors? We need to pray daily: "Let the words of my mouth, and the meditation of my heart, be acceptable in thy sight, O Lord, my strength, and my Redeemer" (Psalm 19:14).

What really is success? In this life we have a tendency to measure it in terms of dollars or position or reputation. That is not the best way to measure success. Some homes are unhappy because a wife has the wrong conception of success. She doesn't understand that success is measured not by just one thing, but by a whole package of things that make up the successful life. Because of this, some wives are constantly complaining about their lot. They live on the wrong side of town, or their car isn't the latest model, or it isn't air-conditioned. . . . They believe that success on the part of their husbands would bring them all of these things. I use the word "things" here because we understand how much that includes. Maybe we are pushing them beyond their abilities.

It is natural to desire a reasonable living. We all want the food and the clothing that is necessary, and a home in which to live. But so often our appetite grows faster than the income, and there is a tendency to push some-body beyond his ability.

It's important for wives to remember that if a man is happy in his work, this should be counted as a great blessing. We should put a very high value on it. Having more things does not necessarily bring happiness. The Scripture says that we should be content with such things as we have.

I would not want you to think that I am so foolish that I do not recognize that there has to be a balance in this. We must not be satisfied with any old thing. We need to be realistic about whether or not our lot in life is favorable. Success that is measured in terms of dollars or things we possess misses its mark completely.

I have a friend who told me about a home in which he stayed when traveling with a singing quartet. He said his host had everything a fellow could want in this world—a wonderful position, a lovely home, a beautiful wife and children, and two nice cars. He thought, *Boy, if I could have what this fellow has, I would be really happy. He must be the happiest man in the country.*

Just before retiring that night, this man said to my friend, "Can I talk to you alone?" My friend said, "Sure." They went out on the porch and this fellow, whom my friend had envied, poured out his heart saying that he was the most miserable person in the world.

He had been a success as far as the world goes, but he didn't know the love of God or real love for his wife. He was on the verge of suicide. My friend was able to point him to the Lord and real happiness.

The measure of success with reference to money

should be, What is being accomplished with the money? Is anyone being helped through the dollars that are entrusted to me? Success is related not to how many dollars we have, but to what we do with the dollars that God has entrusted to us.

When we measure success by the position we have attained, or how high up the ladder of success we have gone, we have missed the point completely. We should rather ask, What am I doing for somebody else through the position that God has permitted me to stand in? The question then is not how much money you have or how high your position. Rather it should be, What are you accomplishing that is worthwhile through these things?

When we give a gift to someone because we feel it is an obligation or we feel that a particular occasion demands it and we are trying to match that gift to the one to whom it is given and his position, no lasting joy comes to us.

When we can give a gift to someone who is in need, or provide something for a person who could not have it otherwise—a permanent at the beauty salon for a missionary, a new dress for your maid, a dinner out for a neighbor who can't afford to go out for dinner—then a much deeper sense of satisfaction comes to us. There is much greater blessing in giving than in receiving. I think the exchange of Christmas gifts is probably the best example of a kind of giving that doesn't bring much satisfaction. In most cases we are giving to those who will also return a gift. There is little joy in this; it's only a chore. We're glad when Christmas is over.

I know of a college professor who somehow has an

127

unusual relationship with the students. They think highly of him, and it is not because he is an easy instructor or one who offers high grades. He is a very exacting teacher, but they know that he has given them a fair grade. They respect him. But the thing that has endeared him to the students is the concern he has for them every day. They feel that he wants to help them. He gives of himself unsparingly.

We began with a consideration of how to have a happy home. I believe if these principles are understood and are practiced, we will find that as spouses and as parents or as both, we will have the greatest happiness. In addition to that, we will have implanted in our sons and daughters the true road to happiness and success in life, because they will understand that it is service to God and service to our fellowman with no expectation of return but only for the joy of doing it that has brought the greatest satisfaction that can come to anyone.

CHAPTER FIFTEEN

SEVEN LETOURNEAUS AND HOW THEY GREW

'TIS God who rules, but not without parents' hands. Whether Mom's methods of raising children were perfect or not, she was at least consistent in her nurturing.

How did the children react to houses full of boarders? Did they resent the public scrutiny? Were they spoiled by having too much money? Following are the stories of Mom's children, the beneficiaries of the spiritual and material wealth handed down by parents who knew no creed but Christ, no law but love, and no better rulebook than the Bible.

SARAH LOUISE

Mom's eldest child, after little Caleb Thomas died in infancy, endured rather than shared her mother's enthusiasm for ministering to boys. Louise fought for acceptance and affirmation in a family dominated by brothers. She had, or thought she had, to win over constantly a father who was of the opinion that "one girl is all you need for housework." Both parents were pleased indeed with Louise when she married a Christian man who entered the family business.

Gus Dick, a graduate of Fletcher College in Iowa, did not always agree with his brothers-in-law and made his opinions known. But he and Louise were ready in 1952 when volunteers were needed to board the flat-bottom LSM and sail to Liberia, Africa, to direct the establishment of Tournata, an experimental missionary station featuring LeTourneau's mighty construction equipment.

With little Evelyn, Robert, and Jeanette, they endured the month-long voyage aboard the flat-bottomed motor vessel until finally the land of their destination rose into sight. R.G. and a crew of men flew to Liberia to help unload the monstrous equipment while Louise and her three children were flown inland to a missionary station.

Enormous responsibilities faced the young woman and her family. They had to set up prefabricated housing, dig a well, install showers, keep from getting malaria, load ironwood and mahogany onto the launch as paying cargo for the trip back to the United States, and build an airstrip.

Three months after they landed, a piece of steel hit Gus's eye. He could not get adequate medical help in time and eventually lost the sight in his left eye.

When an airstrip was built, Mom made a trip to Tournata in the A-26 bomber. Louise gave her a grand tour in the hot, humid port upon which two hundred inches of rain fall every year.

After three years of building and clearing and planting, Gus bid on a fifty-mile road project that the government of Liberia wanted in order to open up the interior. Gus won the contract and found his work load greatly extended.

In May 1956, the Dick family returned to the United States. Three months later Louise gave birth to her fourth child, Joyce Marie. Evelyn was fourteen, so she remained in the United States for high school while the family returned with five-week-old Joyce to Tournata.

In the two years that remained, Gus supervised the completion of the road project before succumbing to malaria and exhaustion. They returned in 1958 to the Midwest where Gus was hired by Deere and Company (builders of John Deere farm equipment) in Moline, Illinois. There Louise raised her family, and there she buried her husband in 1980 when cancer of the bone marrow took his life shortly after he retired in 1979.

Louise spent two years in California but could not find her niche. Her four children were scattered, and she was without roots. In the spring of 1983 she moved to Longview, Texas, where she has been working on a volunteer basis at LeTourneau College to learn computer technology.

"I enjoy the work very much and am feeling more and more at home here," she says.

Louise has four grandsons: Jeffory, Stephan, Wesley, and Ryan.

DONALD PHILLIP

The eldest son of the LeTourneau family proved to be especially difficult to handle, repeating the pattern of

131

his father who, until he was sixteen and converted to Christ, gave his parents plenty of anxious moments.

From the time he could walk, Don seemed bent on mischief. He could be stubborn. One morning he refused to eat his bowl of bran flakes. Mom put the bowl in the refrigerator and served them to him at lunch. Still he wouldn't eat them. She served his bowl of bran flakes at supper, but he went without a meal rather than eat those bran flakes. Not until the following day did he give in and eat the cereal.

Many a night vigil was kept for him; many a car he raced; many a girl he dated. At one point he was determined to marry a girl he had met at Mount Hermon conference grounds near Santa Cruz, California. When his parents were in Hawaii in 1937, where R.G. had been invited to look into the building of a sugar cane harvester, Don drove the family car from Peoria to Stockton, hocking his new overcoat along the way to buy gasoline to make the trip.

The manager of the Stockton plant cabled the LeTourneaus seeking advice. Pop laughed when he heard what Don had done, but Mom cried. They arranged for their son to receive enough money to buy gasoline to get him back to Peoria and to pick up his coat in the pawn shop en route.

The LeTourneaus tried enrolling Don in John Brown University. They tried working their son into the Peoria plant. Not until he met R. A. Forrest, founder of the Toccoa Falls Institute in Georgia, did Don find the path of life that is promised in Psalm 16:11. That glad phone call finally came: "Mom, Dad, I'm saved!" That was followed by the good news that at eighteen he would marry Wilma Morris on graduation day, May 30, 1940.

When his life seemed to be rosiest, Don died at the controls of a light plane over North Carolina. But he had been numbered with the heavenly and will be there to welcome his family to the land of cloudless day some bright morning.

Wilma, his bride, lived for many years near the LeTourneaus in houses provided by them. Later she married Charles Gibson and had a daughter. Wilma died when their daughter was in high school, and her husband has since remarried.

RICHARD HOWARD

The hymn writer noted that a believer's "ordered life" confesses the beauty of God's grace. Such is the example of the fourth LeTourneau heir, the eldest living son.

Richard achieved top grades without agonizing study. As a toddler, he had recovered from the ravages of spinal meningitis through the prayers of his parents. Not only did Richard recover; he has excelled in all of his scholastic and business pursuits. He has always achieved top grades in school without effort. His records, clothing, books, and personal grooming are kept precisely correct, neatly arranged and filed.

"Ask Richard for any photo in his vast files or for any piece of information and he can find it immediately," says his brother Roy.

At eighteen years of age, during World War II, Rich

133

was at the point of being drafted. He wanted to join the flight training program but the LeTourneau plants needed the young man to carry blueprints to their Sydney, Australia, operation and help the engineers there to properly interpret the specifications on mechanical drawings that were dispatched. Rich was familiar with each product and could help the Australians translate specifications to their metric system of calculation.

From New York he sailed the treacherous wartime seas in the winter of 1943, turning nineteen on-board ship somewhere at sea on January 3, 1944.

He sailed on a ship that had joined a caravan of vessels for safety, across the Caribbean, through the Panama Canal, and across the South Pacific to Melbourne in forty-nine days.

After Rich had fulfilled his mission for the company, the Selective Service decreed that his time had come to be drafted. In July, 1944, Rich enlisted and was sent to a replacement depot in Brisbane. The U.S. Army was mobilizing for the invasion into the Philippines.

Rich traveled in uniform to New Guinea where he was assigned to light maintenance, working out of a truck with a full machine shop installed in its bed. He arrived in the Philippines fourteen days behind the initial invasion and never saw combat.

After October 1944, when General Douglas MacArthur made good his promise and returned to the Philippines, Rich got a pass and flew on military planes back to Australia. His military company later went to Japan and finally was returned to the States.

Rich was eighteen when he left home and twenty-one when he returned. Mom treasures yet his colorful letters about the people he met, about his experiences down under, and about his experiences in the war that was to make the world safe for democracy.

Today Rich is president of LeTourneau College, presiding over a thriving educational enterprise for which his mother first had the vision in 1946. He married Louise Jensen in 1947. They have four children: Robert Gilmore, Jr., Caleb, Linda, and Liela. Both of their daughters were adopted in infancy. They have six grandchildren: Kimberly, Robert G. III, Krista, Rene, Jason, and Charis.

ROY SAMUEL

Like all the other children, Roy was born in Stockton, California, his birthday falling on April 21, 1929. At the age of six, he moved to Peoria, Illinois, in his family's great relocation. Thereafter he was enrolled in four schools in the span of five years.

Roy (most like his mother's side in looks, his dad's in a lot of other ways) started working in the LeTourneau plant at the age of ten as an electric arc welder. He spent all of his vacations, summers, Christmases—every chance he could get—welding metal.

After one year at Toccoa Falls Institute in Georgia, he moved to Vicksburg, Mississippi, to be with his parents. As a high school freshman in Vicksburg County High School, he would go to work in the engineering department as a draftsman from 7:00 A.M. until 9:00 A.M. After attending class from 9:00 A.M. until 12:30

P.M., he would eat lunch and work the rest of the afternoon until 6:00 P.M. as a machinist in his father's plant.

He was graduated in 1947 from the Wheaton Academy in Illinois. During that summer he earned his pilot's license.

One year later Roy entered Texas A & M University as a freshman, then returned to the plant for the summer, in charge of the experimental department.

Early in 1951, at the age of twenty-two, he traveled back to his roots in California and met Shirley Stanfield. She became his wife in August of that year.

On a return flight with his dad from Liberia in the late 1950s, R.G. showed his son a letter inviting LeTourneau to build a road in the jungles of Peru. That spring, Roy and Shirley flew with R.G. to Lima and on to Pucallpa in the Peruvian jungle to have a look. Roy signed a contract shortly thereafter to build thirty-five miles of road through the jungle. In return, the government was to give LeTourneau a million acres of land. Roy's intentions were to develop the land, colonize it, and sell it to recoup LeTourneau's investment.

The road was built with LeTourneau's monster earth-and-tree-moving equipment and a thriving community established. Tournavista thrived. It marked the beginning of a missionary enterprise that Roy directs today. A herd of about five thousand beef cattle was built up after the road was completed. Roy moved his family to Lima, Peru's capital, and lived there for nearly five years to direct the Tournavista enterprise. They returned to the United States in 1961.

The LeTourneau enterprise by that year had fallen

into financial difficulties. R.G. appointed Roy executive vice-president of the corporation. Key management consultants managed to raise enough money to put the company back on a firm financial footing.

While still looking after the Peru projects, Roy finished school at North Texas State University, majoring in business administration. He later went into business with his brother Ben by purchasing John Deere Industrial Equipment dealerships in Orlando, Tampa, and Ocala, Florida. They became John Deere's largest dealerships in the nation.

The John Deere dealership was sold in January 1975. A month later, Roy bought an airplane dealership. The gasoline shortage cut into the business drastically. During the economic recession of 1976 Roy saw his company move to within hours of bankruptcy. When the business was finally turned over to another investor, Roy and Shirley bought a motor home and went on a two-month vacation back to California, up to Seattle, and finally to Rockwall, Texas, to visit friends. There Roy entered into the residential construction business and set up the headquarters of the LeTourneau Foundation, raising money for missionary projects in South America through LeTourneau Ministries International. He serves also as international chairman of Christian Business Men's Committee.

Their children are Brenda, secretary and treasurer of the Foundation; Nancy, in training for her Master's degree in family counseling; Donald, a counselor in social work in Minneapolis; and Randy, earning a degree in computer science and working for Roy in the LeTourneau Foundation office.

TED LORIMER

Mom's sixth child died on December 19, 1982, at the age of fifty. He was most like R.G., a genius of sorts in electrical and mechanical engineering.

In 1949, at seventeen, Ted was riding a motorcycle on a Longview street when it slammed into an automobile. Both his legs, an arm, and his jaw were broken. The accident also gave him a bad concussion and damaged his liver.

Mom was the only one at home when Ted suffered the accident. She stayed at the side of her son's hospital bed on Friday night and all day Saturday. The doctor finally persuaded her to go home on the second night and get some rest. At 2:00 A.M. he phoned, "Better come, Mom. I don't think he'll make it."

Mom called Pop and Roy in Minnesota, Louise and Gus in Nebraska, and Rich in Vicksburg. The family gathered, but Ted pulled through. He was unconscious for a week. For twelve months he struggled to get well. Doctors broke all of his damaged bones again in order to allow them to heal properly.

In May 1953, Ted was married to Joyce Davenport of Longview. The couple had three boys—Mike, Tom, and Scott.

In 1977 Ted returned to school at Texas A & M. He was graduated two years later and taught school at LeTourneau for two and half years. From 1979 on he battled illness until on December 19, 1982, he slipped into a coma and went to be with his Lord.

BEN WALTER

Ben Walter was born on March 21, 1934, during the great economic depression. The seventh child of the LeTourneaus, he is known as the guy who can own a dollar longer than any of the clan. Ben, like all of the LeTourneau children, never received an allowance from his parents. The children had to work for whatever money they wanted.

Ben moved with the family to Peoria, Illinois, as a baby of one year. Subsequently he lived in Toccoa, Georgia, then in Mississippi, and finally in Longview, Texas, where he resides with his wife and their three children.

In the seventh grade Ben met Bettye Locker and never dated another girl until he married her six years later.

He finished high school in three years and received an Associate of Arts degree from LeTourneau College while working full-time at the LeTourneau factory. For two years he worked until 2:30 A.M. every day and also attended school. As a nineteen-year-old groom he became a tool and die maker at his father's plant. Later he set up the production facility to manufacture one hundred-pound bombs in the Longview factory.

He took this experience to the Vicksburg facility in 1954, where he supervised the production of bombs weighing up to one thousand pounds. At twenty he was the general manager of the Mississippi factory, which employed eight hundred people, holding that position for thirteen years. It was Ben who started the LeTourneau company in the production of offshore oil-drilling rigs. He directed the building of the first mobile jack-up type of drilling platform and eventually built more than thirty platforms costing ten million dollars each. Those rigs are now at work in Alaska, the North Sea, along the coast of France, Japan, Arabia, South America, the Gulf of Mexico, and in many other parts of the world.

In 1967 Ben was transferred to Longview to become overseer of all the LeTourneau factories, then employing some three thousand people.

A leave of absence followed so he could earn a degree at Texas A & M University, where he graduated with a Bachelor's degree in industrial engineering. His grade point average put Ben in the top 10 percent of his class.

After his 1970 graduation, when the LeTourneau factories were sold, he teamed with his brother Roy to form the LeTourneau Tractor Company in Orlando, Tampa, and Ocala, Florida to represent the John Deere Industrial Division for central Florida. In five years those outlets grew to become John Deere's largest dealerships in the world.

When the economy declined in 1975, the company was sold and Ben returned to Longview to assist brother Richard, president of LeTourneau College.

Later that year Ben and his wife and a sister-in-law started the Camera, Hobbycraft World, Inc., which now has three retail outlets. The work is far removed from the iron industry in which Ben was raised, but he views it as another opportunity "to do the best job we know how with whatever God gives us to do."

Ben and Bettye had four children: Sherrye Alyce, Mark Alden, Roy Walter, and Janine Joy.

"In 1982," says Ben, "the Lord took our son Roy Walter home to be with him. This was the most difficult time of our lives. I had accepted Christ as my Savior at the age of ten. Especially since my marriage, we have tried to live for him. We have held loosely to our possessions. But not until the Lord took our son did we realize exactly what God expects of us—a full commitment, even to the extent that we should be willing to give up a child whom we dearly loved."

As a double blow, one week later that December in 1982, Ben lost his brother Ted, a man just two years older, to whom he had been the closest among his siblings.

The eldest daughter of Ben and Bettye, Sherrye Alyce, directs her own music company, singing and playing the piano as she serves God with talent and voice.

Mark Alden married Deborah George. They have given Ben and Bettye three grandchildren: Dawn Amee, Mark Anthony, and Adam Lee. Mark, in business with his parents, expects to enter the full-time Christian ministry.

Janine Joy, their youngest child, has married Joel Hedgpeth; they have one child, Melissa Nicole. (Mom says, "Melissa is R.G.'s Baby's Baby's Baby—Ben is my baby, Janine is his baby, and Melissa is her baby.")

Ben is going strong at half a century, desiring to serve God wherever and at whatever task he presents.

CHAPTER SIXTEEN

BEYOND TODAY

A closing message from Mom LeTourneau

THE joy of anticipation is a big part of the Christian experience. There are fewer deaths in retirement homes during holiday celebrations and other special occasions because older people anticipate the joy of being with the people they love. Anticipation tones up the whole system. It might be the extra energy you feel when you make the house ready for a party, or for the visit of a son or daughter, or for a friend. It might be the joy of celebrating good fortune or sudden blessings of a hundred different kinds.

A child knows the keen delight of anticipation perhaps more than we adults. To express their enthusiasm for a coming event they jump up and down, clap their hands, cheer and gurgle with delight. God asks us to be "like a little child" in our approach to his salvation. We know so little of his mighty works, we are so slow to believe, and we are blind to many beautiful serendipities that he brings into our lives to bless and inspire.

For this book I have looked back a long way. The words of a song come to me as I think of all that has happened since November 15, 1900, when I first breathed the air of this earth:

When all thy mercies, O my God,
My wondering soul surveys,
Transported with that view I'm lost
In wonder, love, and praise.

No one knows the day or the hour when our work on this earth will be finished. That is as it should be. God has put into each heart the desire to live. Only the disturbed mind considers destroying that life.

To make life meaningful, we must always be moving toward an objective. Without a goal, life becomes oppressive.

When my husband was asked which year of his life was the best, he would always answer, "The next one." Right up to the time of his death he was planning for the future. He did not look back and gloat over past accomplishments, or lament the discouraging bad times that were also part of his life.

Many, like me, are suffering the deteriorations of age and crippling conditions. These agonies can be very real. I do not speak of them lightly. But all of us need to be aware lest we lose our enthusiasm for the future. If we do, we will miss the beauty and the blessings of life that God gives us every day.

144

I am as old as the twentieth century, and I may live to the very end of it. God knows the physical and moral strength that I need when care weighs me down. He promises in Hebrews 13:5, "I will never leave thee, nor forsake thee."

The Bible encourages each believer to put energy and drive into daily living. "Whatsoever thy hand findeth to do, do it with thy might" (Eccles. 9:10). And, "Whatsoever ye do, do it heartily, as to the Lord, and not unto men" (Col. 3:23).

What gives more joy than tackling a difficult task and accomplishing the goal of completing it? The Apostle Paul wrote that he put the past out of his mind and pressed on toward the goal of his life. That goal was "the prize of the high calling of God in Christ Jesus." He could endure *all* things and was *persuaded,* based upon the promises of God. He knew that nothing could separate him from the love of God and that he was secure.

During a recent medical checkup, a test revealed a tumor the size of a golf ball growing in my colon. I was home a week after the surgery, resting comfortably and thankful to be back with my family and friends in my own house. The most wonderful part of the entire experience, which interrupted my routine, was the wonderful peace that God gave me through it all. I was not even upset when the doctor told me it was cancer.

"If it is time for me to go, fine," I said. "But if the Lord has something yet for me to do, that's fine too."

After a walk of many years with the Lord, I want to state that my faith in him has grown stronger. Like the

Apostle Paul, I know that "all things work together for good to them that love God, to them who are the called according to his purpose."

Praise the Lord.